Homeless

Homeless

true stories
of life on the streets

Andrew Byrne

NEW
HOLLAND

First published in Australia in 2005 by
New Holland Publishers (Australia) Pty Ltd
Sydney • Auckland • London • Cape Town

14 Aquatic Drive Frenchs Forest NSW 2086 Australia
218 Lake Road Northcote Auckland New Zealand
86 Edgware Road London W2 2EA United Kingdom
80 McKenzie Street Cape Town 8001 South Africa

National Library of Australia Cataloguing-in-Publication Data:

Byrne, Andrew, 1971- .
Homeless : true stories of life on the streets

ISBN 1 74110 212 X.

1. Homeless persons - New South Wales - Sydney - Biography.
2. Homelessness - New South Wales - Sydney. 3. Sydney
(N.S.W.) - Social conditions. I. Title.

305.5692099441

Managing Editor: Monica Berton
Project Editor: Jacqueline Blanchard
Designer: Karlman Roper
Production Contoller: Kellie Matterson
Printed in Australia by McPherson's Printing Group, Victoria

10 9 8 7 6 5 4 3 2 1

Acknowledgements

This book is the result of the kindness, support, generosity and understanding of many individuals. I would like to thank:

Jay, Chris Strauss, Dave Wilson, Davina Coad, Davo Marsh, Henry Thompson, Jai, John McDonald, Josephine, Liam, Linz, Mike Reeves, Nathan, Ray Brown, Ray Sippel, Ricky Cain, Sallie, Terry Balmer, Todd Parker and Tom 'Animal' Lee. Each of you were not only gratefully willing to tell me your story, but gave me the opportunity to speak with some of the most inspiring and wisest people I've ever met. It was a privilege and an education. I wish each of you the contentedness and security you deserve.

Mekonen Lemma, Danny, Edwidge, Graciela and Marcia at The Station Ltd. Drop-in Centre; Laurie, Jane, Stephanie, Mike, Jai and Luis at Rough Edges Community Centre; Phyllis and Josephine at the Mac Silva Centre; Jackie and Aaron at Twenty10 Gay and Lesbian Youth Centre. Your strength of character, dedication and compassion deeply impressed and touched me. In a sensible world, people such as you would be hailed heroic. In this world you simply are heroic.

The many homeless men and women who I spoke with while researching this book. Like those appearing in these pages, you opened up a world I'd seen but never really knew—humanity.

The various counsellors, social workers and volunteers working in the numerous centres, shelters and kitchens, particularly; Our Lady of the Snows, Vincentian Village and Matt Talbot. Special thanks to St Paul's Mission for the coffee and pizza, too. And also Ben Nacard, for opening the curtain to my first day of field research. Cheers, mate.

The wonderful staff at New Holland. Thanks to Fiona Schultz, for believing in the worth of this project and for your advice and uplifting support. Jacqueline Blanchard, for your outstanding editing capabilities, hard work, wisdom, advice, patience and heart. Also Robynne Millward, for giving me the first opportunity that led to this project.

Father Chris Riley and Lord Mayor of the City of Sydney, Clover Moore, for very kindly contributing their experience, insight, time and words to this book. Also, Judy Gorton and Roy Bishop for your much appreciated time and efforts.

My family and friends dotted across Australia, Ireland and Luxembourg. What can I say? Your encouragement and advice, wisdom and love over the years and throughout this book have nourished my life immeasurably.

Angela Tam and Zoe Slater for your support, belief, friendship, humour, advice and love. I offer you my own love and gratitude in return.

To those in the quiet background—mitakuye oyasin.

Finally and deeply, thank you Lin. Your strength and beautiful sunlight love has always been a source of inspiration, encouragement and refined harmony to me. I'm honoured by your insightfulness, intelligence, gypsy femininity, wicked sense of humour, unique creativity and passion. Thanks for your patience, support, the driving, the late-night coffees and hugs while I worked on this book. Life is good—I love you.

Foreword

A truly civil society would ensure that homeless people get the help they need to get back on their feet. It is a sad fact that this does not occur in Australia.

According to the Australian Council of Social Services, housing is now at its least affordable, and during the last decade:

- Average house prices relative to household income have almost doubled;
- The proportion of first homebuyers has fallen by about 30%;
- Average monthly payments on new loans have increased by 50%;
- The proportion of low-rent homes has fallen by about 15%;
- Opportunities to rent public housing have been cut by 20%;

- More than 100 families with children are turned away each night from emergency refuges.

Inner Sydney, like other urban centres in Australia, has a disproportionate number of homeless people, many of whom are drawn from suburban and rural areas. They are predominantly young adults, with a slight majority of males.

Homelessness is caused by many factors. It is a bottom-line indicator of how well the public safety net provides for people in our community. The rise in homelessness reflects a complex interplay of factors, including the growing gap between rich and poor, high youth unemployment and government policies promoting urban consolidation.

Some 75% of clients of homelessness services suffer at least one mental disorder, compared with only 18% of the general population. Without proper treatment many end up in prison, then back on the streets when released. A further 50% are likely to have an alcohol or drug problem, and more than 90% of homeless people suffer from chronic health conditions such as asthma and diabetes.

Successive governments have failed to replace large mental institutions with adequate community care for people suffering from mental illness. De-institutionalisation has left the bulk of responsibility for supporting them to families and carers, placing huge stress on communities and leaving many people homeless.

Substance and gambling addiction, a history of abuse and neglect, family breakdowns and lack of education all contribute to homelessness. It is easy to understand how a homeless person might miss out on vital living skills. If they have been homeless for a long time and formed a community on the street, moving into a 'proper home' may be too isolating for them to contemplate or sustain.

Homeless people are more likely to be excluded from many of society's benefits and become 'invisible' to other residents. Homeless people have complex and varied needs. They require well-resourced services that can address the underlying causes of homelessness and help them get and maintain accommodation, providing homeless people with long-term support while it's needed.

Despite longstanding evidence of need, mental health services remain drastically under-resourced and totally inadequate for people who have both a mental illness and an alcohol or drug problem (Dual Diagnosis). Our health services focus on treating only one problem, while people with a number of concerns, who are most in need of intensive help, are sent on a merry-go-round between services because their situation and needs are complex.

There also needs to be a clear pathway for homeless people to move from the street, to regain their place in the mainstream. Projects that help people make this transition are critical to help homeless people get back on their feet, including appropriate training and jobs. Extra effort is needed to ensure a long-term focus on employment, enterprise and mentoring to help them stay on their feet.

Good mental health, family support, as well as alcohol and drug services, are fundamental to preventing homelessness. Because homelessness is one of those issues that is likely to always be with us, despite our best efforts, we need services that can effectively reach out to homeless people who have been alienated. Outreach services for homeless people on the street and help to re-build relationships are essential.

Homelessness is a national problem and requires national responses. The Commonwealth Government has to take serious action to prevent homelessness and improve housing affordability. State and Territory Governments and service providers can make sure that adequate support services reach those in need.

All this will require a significant shift in government priorities and enormous pressure from the whole community. I urge readers to speak up about this need, talk to your representatives, to make sure that homeless people have a voice and don't remain invisible.

Clover Moore MP
Member for Bligh
Lord Mayor of Sydney

Contents

I had three chairs in my house; one for solitude,
two for friendship, three for society.

—*Henry David Thoreau (1817–1862)*

Introduction

We've all walked past or seen a homeless person and wondered, at some point, what their story is. Who are they? How did they become homeless? What does life like look through their eyes? What is it like to not have a home?

Over a period of four months I met with twenty currently and previously homeless people in Sydney (primarily in the inner-city area) and asked them to speak openly about their lives, their experiences and their thoughts on homelessness. The result is this book: a collection of their stories and views in their own words.

When I began this project I thought I had a fair understanding of homelessness; its causes, its characters, its community and its culture. I quickly found that the homeless community operated in a world varyingly out of phase with what most people call 'everyday life'. A great deal of what I knew (and thought I knew) about homeless culture was turned upside down. I was in for one hell of an education.

Introduction

From the start, I wanted to put together a book that would be read by the general public and not just those primarily involved in the issue of homelessness, such as social workers, charity workers or academics. This book is not intended as an academic analysis or overview of homelessness in Australia; it is an illustrative account of the homeless experience from those who have lived it or still are living it.

I began my research by reading through much of what has been written by government and welfare organisations through the years on the subject. I also spoke with people working with the homeless, such as social workers and volunteers. Firstly, I wanted to get a firm understanding of homelessness, an overview of its background and history. Secondly, I needed a realistic definition of homelessness to provide a basis for my research. Exactly what characteristics define somebody as being homeless?

Understandably, much of what has been written on the subject is intended to assist government and welfare organisations in developing strategies and approaches. However, outside of notable publications such as *The Big Issue* magazine, there is little widely available to the general public to explain or describe homelessness on a very human and personal level, which is what this book aims to do.

Homelessness seems to have become a debate between different groups, each one trying to deal with the problem with their own agenda—and generally with insufficient funds or resources. Homelessness is not an issue unto itself; it cuts across areas such as domestic violence, sexual abuse, substance abuse, gambling, mental health, family breakdown and poverty. Each of these social

Introduction

issues is covered separately by numerous government departments and welfare and interest groups. This overlap has meant that multiple views and agendas, no matter how necessary, valid or well-intentioned, have been thrown into the discussion. As a result, to get a thorough definition of homelessness it is a case of 'it depends on who you ask'.

In the end, the definition I chose for my work came from the Australian Institute of Health and Welfare. They classed a homeless person as someone who is:

- currently living on the street;
- living in crisis or refuge accommodation;
- living in temporary arrangements without security of tenure, for example, moving between residences of friends or relatives, living in squats, caravans or improvised dwellings, or living in boarding houses;
- living in unsafe family circumstances, for example, families in which child abuse or domestic violence is a threat or has occurred;
- living on very low incomes and facing extraordinary expenses or personal crisis.[1]

I also set research guidelines for each interview. First and foremost, I wanted to ensure that I always respected the dignity and privacy of each person I interviewed. As a result, some people's names have been changed to protect their identity and to respect the privacy of their families and friends. In some cases, they requested not to be photographed for similar reasons.

Introduction

In the interests of accuracy and respecting each contributor (and the reader), I was extremely careful not to filter or alter the meaning of each person's words when I transcribed them. It is very easy for a writer to edit someone else's words and consciously or unconsciously alter what that person meant to say. So, every word and sentence was carefully transferred from tape to written word. Each contributor was also given the chance to review the completed story. Unfortunately, in a few cases, the person had moved on or could not be found. In these cases I tried everything I could to contact those who had essentially vanished. I sought them at their last known locations and tried tracking them via other homeless people they knew, shelters, drop-in centres, and a lot of footwork. I soon learned that this characteristic 'vanishing' of some people in the homeless community came with the territory. It was one part of the overall education I received in those four months of interviews; an education discussed in more detail in the postscript.

As for the interviews themselves, I needed to find people who were willing and able to tell their story. At first, I decided to search randomly on the streets. This method proved to be generally unworkable for a couple of reasons. Firstly, many were wary of a stranger coming up to them in the street and as a result were not keen to be interviewed. Secondly, in some cases, the person was suffering from varying degrees of mental illness or drug or alcohol intoxication, making it simply impractical (and unfair) to attempt or finish an interview. For some people, discussing their past was emotionally stressful. This was not the situation with all cases, but it occurred enough to make me realise that I needed to try a better, less haphazard approach to finding people to interview.

Introduction

So, after nearly a month of trying the random approach I began contacting homeless shelters and drop-in centres, explaining the project and asking for permission to use their organisation as a middle ground. All of these groups were clear about their desire to protect their clients and many turned me down for those reasons. This was especially the case for women's shelters, where many of their clients were still at risk of spousal violence and understandably reticent to be interviewed.

Whether my request was turned down or accepted, I respect the fact that these social workers and counsellors were acting in the best interests of the homeless they worked with. In the end, most of the interviews were gained through four main drop-in centres in and around Sydney:

- The Station Ltd Drop-in Centre and Housing Development Program in the Sydney CBD;
- Rough Edges Community Centre in Darlinghurst;
- Mac Silva Centre (Aboriginal men's shelter) in Waterloo; and
- Twenty10 Gay and Lesbian Youth Support in Newtown.

Each organisation provides a place for the homeless to feel safe, have a meal, wash, seek counselling and obtain help in finding accommodation. The efforts of many of these workers go unheard of in the public arena and that is a shame. Despite limited funding, high workloads and a constant flow of new and ongoing cases, they still manage to help people put their lives back together.

To provide a personal view of the environment that people from these organisations work within, I invited Chris Riley to offer a commentary. Father Riley has put in a tremendous effort over the years via his Youth Off The Streets programs. His commentary, on pages 21–24, is a series of excerpts taken from his own journal.

The people I interviewed in this book were equally giving of themselves. They volunteered their story to someone they knew nothing about. I always made it clear that if there was anything they didn't want written, they could either tell me at the time or it could be deleted later. Although as a writer I knew this might cause problems in presenting a full account of their story, I again wanted to maintain a respect for their privacy and for them to trust me with their words. Consequently, I was humbled and incredibly grateful that virtually all of the people I interviewed were open and frank about their pasts and their views.

The interviews were conducted on the streets, in drop-in and referral centres and at the current abodes or workplaces of one or two of the interviewees. I tried to make the interviews as relaxed and conversational as possible. The actual interview recordings took from thirty minutes to a couple of hours. I asked people to speak about where they came from and what led to their homelessness. I wanted to find out what the homeless experience looks like through their eyes.

As they spoke, I often had to remind myself that what I was hearing was something the person sitting with me had gone through or was going through. Their stories lifted the lid on a world that we in the general public have little or no idea of. Not just what people experience on the streets, but the causes that led to them being there, the lives they led before and the effects that homelessness had on them.

Introduction

From the beginning, I intended the interviews to be on a voluntary basis only and expected that the people I spoke with would want to be involved based on the merits of the project alone; that is, to give the general public a personal understanding of homelessness. This was twinned with the understanding that they would not be paid for their story, as occurs in the news media. It was a difficult decision to make but I felt it was necessary to avoid any perception of 'cash for comment' and the like.

However; in the interests of honesty, and after seeking advice on this from a veteran social worker with the homeless, I did give $20 as a token gift to each contributor for taking time to record the interview. This occurred with the very first person I interviewed and I decided to keep it on as a kind of tradition, ensuring that each interviewee was treated equally.

I must also point out that the $20 was only mentioned after the interview, not before. In most cases, people did not want to take the money, as they were supportive of the project's aims. For me this was almost as awkward as not giving a token at all; I did not want to offend their pride either. In some cases people donated their $20 to charity, so we could both walk away feeling better about it!

At the same time, considering this book is about the homeless, it would be equally ignoble for the writer to take money for it. One hundred per cent of the author's fees (advance and royalties) are being donated directly to those homeless drop-in and referral centres that assisted in the creation of this book.

It is my hope that these stories help shed light on a crisis that some 100,000[2] homeless Australians are living in today. The people you are about to hear from ended up homeless for various reasons

Introduction

and suffered it in varying degrees. While they share the common experience of homelessness, there is another commonality they share with you and me—we're all members of the same public.

—Andrew Byrne

Father Chris Riley on working on the streets

Father Chris Riley has been working to help troubled teenagers for thirty years. Since 1991, his Youth Off The Streets organisation has helped thousands of young Australians through its outreach, food van and refuge programs along with Sydney's only (non-medicated) detox centre. The following commentary is taken from a series of Father Riley's journal entries.

27 April

The wind was cold and I could feel the winter setting in. Not many kids tonight, as many had been locked up. I noticed one of them on the bench so I thought I would wake him up for a feed. I was surprised to find Barry (I thought he was in lock-up). I tried to wake him, but it was difficult. He was shivering and kicking the bench in spasms. I knew he could sort of hear me but also knew he was not really conscious. I tried to make sense of his mumblings and could only gather that he was saying that he was cold. He clutched his shoulders. I asked him if he wanted something to eat to warm him up, but he said, 'It doesn't matter.' The tragedy of his situation hit me. It was an all points low—I ached inside to see a human being shivering and cold, expecting nothing.

These are truly the poor of God—the ones we see so often judged by our middle-class values, but if we saw them in God's light, I wonder who the outcasts would really be.

I realised that people may judge me harshly because I had aligned myself with the homeless.

May 5

The word was that they're all fighting. Julie was out of lock-up and stirring up trouble. She punched Paul in the mouth, who was rolling drunk. Paul walked over to me with blood pouring from his mouth. He said something to me, then something 'clacked', he punched my car's window and then ran for a guy on the footpath, grabbed him in a head lock and threw him to the ground. Several of us grabbed Paul and released his innocent victim. Eventually he calmed down as I knelt on the ground next to him. An elderly man walked past and said, 'Father, please get up! You're demeaning yourself.' I told him I didn't think I was.

I realised that when you align yourself with the poor, others will see you as crazy and misdirected.

The homeless live in a world that most people could not imagine.

May 10

I met up with three kids who were coming to the basketball at the Entertainment Centre. When I entered the stadium I realised what a different world I had moved into. As we sat down, people stared at us. I realised that the kids really stank. I hadn't realised it was so bad, as we were usually outside. They started to swear at the referees. Again people gave these sideward glances and some got up and moved. I was a bit uncomfortable, but I soon realised that these kids are worlds apart from the average Australian. I realised that I have opted to live and work with the underclass, and this will certainly bring to me a great deal of pain and misunderstanding. I was proud to be with them.

As play went on and the crowd interacted with the band, the kids giggled and laughed like little kids. The whole atmosphere enchanted them. They cheered and yelled out in unison with the crowd, and the whole time they were open-eyed. Probably the first time they had ever been to something like this. Many things we take for granted have never been given to these kids. The normal experience of childhood has been ripped from them by violence, sexual abuse and rejection.

The homeless live in an underworld and are confronted with pain and death every day of their lives.

June 6

What do you do when one of them tells you that he has murdered someone? I wonder if it is the alcohol talking? I feel powerless and confused as I listened to the kid's story. He talks of pills being forced onto the young, who are then raped. Tears come gushing from his eyes, so he tells me of a young thirteen-year-old boy who was raped and now works as a male prostitute and is a heroin addict. I conclude that while I am touching the lives of many young people at Town Hall, the problem is bigger. Street kids form an underground population, many living on the edge of life and death. Who knows what pain is being experienced, who knows how many kids disappear and are never found.

I was confronted very powerfully with their pain and their destruction. I begin to realise that many things will be revealed to me and I will not be able to do much about it.

The amount of violence on the streets is heartbreaking. The homeless live in constant fear of being attached. These kids are soft, sensitive, caring and loyal—but also brutal.

Sallie
age 35

I grew up in country NSW on a 10 000-acre farm and lived there up until I went to a co-ed boarding school, which was really good fun for a teenager. I got a new stepdad when I was seven. He used to visit my sisters and me in the night and that's why I ended up going to a boarding school, to get away from him. I'd complained to my mother about my stepdad's abuse and nothing happened. Then I complained to my grandmother. Two weeks later I went to boarding school.

Before I went to boarding school, at twelve years old, I fell pregnant to my stepdad and I ended up having a boy but I wasn't able to keep him. [When my son grew up and we spoke] the hardest part was explaining it to him. He took it really well when I explained [that] I gave him up because I was twelve, and because of who his father was. He had really good adoptive parents and he's now married with two kids of his own. It's a bit rough finding out at thirty that you're a grandmother! But other than that, it was pretty cool meeting him. He still wants to meet his father, but I just can't be the one that does it.

At boarding school I got into pot [marijuana] and amphetamines, but that was only at the weekends. When I left school I got a job in nursing doing palliative care, which made me constantly depressed. I started smoking even more pot and using more amphetamines. That was when I was around twenty years old.

About that time I had a boyfriend and [one day] he was supposed to go get some speed [amphetamine] and when he comes back—it wasn't until I had the needle stuck in my arm—he turns around and says, 'I couldn't get speed, I got heroin.' And that was my first experience of heroin.

I wasn't expecting this high buzz and I ended up doped to the eyeballs for almost two days from that first shot, not being used to heroin at all. The first day I don't remember shit. The second day I was nauseous and sick. I don't know how I ever used it again. But then I started using now and again; the buzz was really good. Every now and again, I got more confident. It got to [where I was using heroin] every day and then two or three times a day; and then suddenly there's no money left in the bank and the rent hadn't been paid for months.

It didn't hit home until the first eviction. I lived with my grandparents for a couple of months and after that I moved into a flat with my brother and we all ended up getting kicked out of there. After the eviction I just threw my job in because I just couldn't work with death any more. It didn't worry me about my [heroin] habit or whatever; I just couldn't work with death any more.

Sallie

I'd go and see people, friends, in the Cross [Kings Cross]. I was staying at my friend's house, but when I was going to the Cross and speeding off my head for days anyway, there was no need to find accommodation. After a couple of years of that you soon start getting sick of it. Then you start staying at a couple of parks and you get thrown out of them.

The first time I slept out, there was a group of us who'd been awake for five or six days and we sort of camped in this park and I just slept. It was the most uncomfortable, annoying experience. Unfortunately, it just got easier to live with; I eventually got used to it.

We stayed at various parks in the Cross and various churches like St Canice's, Wayside Chapel, St John's, Sacred Heart. We stayed under the pergola in Green Park. If you were in the park the automatic sprinklers would start at six o'clock, so you've got to be up before then. We had a tent set up at the park in Rushcutters Bay, which was amazing. We were at the grandstand in front of the oval, and there were the tennis courts down there, and they did not want us there! Eventually the rangers moved us on because some idiot started getting a campfire going. We were alright until then. We also stayed in Woolloomooloo at the navy car park. [The authorities] have since put fences under the bridges, and various churches have taken awnings and seating away so people don't sleep there.

I ended up falling pregnant at twenty-one and having a baby, Anthony. I got my act together for most of that; I was only using every now and again. At that stage, me and Anthony were staying with a friend who had a Department of Housing place. Anthony

Sallie

was going to preschool four days a week. I was back in tech, in school; my life was coming together. I had all the paperwork approved to get a home with the Department of Housing, until he went away to [his] grandma. I had Anthony for his first four years, until he went to his grandmother for a two-week holiday—he's fourteen now [and currently in the custody of my stepsister and stepfather].

He [Anthony] knows I'm here if he ever needs me, and if he ever wants to come and live with me, he knows he can. There's an empty spot that's always there [inside] and some days are harder, especially coming up to his birthday. He'd gone for a holiday and never come back. My mum just said, 'Sign the custody papers or he's not coming home.' Even when I did sign them, he wasn't coming home.

That sort of sent me off the rails again. I went on a huge heroin binge for four months and got my habit back. I'd used up all my savings and all of the money I'd gotten from a compo [compensation] claim when I got hit by a car when I was fifteen—I didn't get that until I was twenty-two. That was $200,000; it was all gone in four months. I had a lot of friends to help me [spend it] though. Mind you, not many of them were still around after the money was gone.

I've seen Anthony twice in the last ten years. I've had phone calls with him regularly. It really kills me, because Anthony's not doing well at school and he's got himself expelled. But there's nothing I can do for him [because of the custody].

After I'd lost him, I was staying with old friends here and there and sleeping with some of them occasionally to get what I wanted.

Sallie

That went on and off for the next few years. By that stage I was need-ing an income for my heroin and I sort of drifted into prostitution.

I started off in massage parlours, then brothels, and then I went to work on the streets because with a massage parlour [the pay] was a sixty–forty split. A brothel was an eighty–twenty split. When I went working on the street, it was one hundred per cent [my own].

A friend of mine knew I needed money and introduced me to a lady that worked in a massage parlour. So I went for an interview with her and she just asked me, 'Have you ever massaged?' She gave me the job that day—apparently I had nice strong hands.

The massage itself wasn't great money but there was extras you could do with the job and you could earn good money from that. That's how I ended up moving into a brothel. I worked in a couple of bondage parlours for a while—that was excellent money. It was a different clientele and there were a lot of different services you could do, not just screwing. I didn't find it difficult. I've got no problem bashing men! I [always] thought each to their own, 'cause I was always the one in control of that situation, so they never actually hurt me. I could massage a guy for half an hour with my stiletto heels for $600 every three days!

I worked in the massage industry for five years. At the same time I was doing courier work for a drug dealer bringing kilos and kilos of stuff from Brisbane and Melbourne. That was more scary 'cause I knew there was more gaol time involved, but it was also my choice. I did five trips all up, but I never got caught. The money was enough that you didn't want to touch what you were courier-ing. The scene was too dangerous to be involved in, though, and it

Sallie

was so hard to get myself out of it. It was mostly amphetamines. A lot of the bikies steer clear of the heroin.

I stopped working for those guys and had to lay low for a while, so I went up to Darwin. That is the most boring place on earth for the drug scene! I stayed up there for three months and came back. Then we did some fruit-picking up and the down the east coast for eighteen months. There's a couple of things I'm not doing again; pineapples, asparagus, strawberries—they're too near the ground. I've done grapes, apples, oranges; I'm just never doin' pineapples, asparagus or strawberries again! I don't eat asparagus and it took me five years to get over strawberries.

Afterwards, I drifted back to Sydney, back to the Cross. Once you're in the Cross you always end up drifting back to it. These days I'm in there four days a week working at St Canice's and I'm not missing anything; I don't want to go back to it [living on the streets and doing heroin].

The worst thing about being homeless up the Cross was the 'tourists' that come up from western Sydney. They used to come and throw eggs at us. One of them threw a couple of Molotov cocktails and set a couple of people's sleeping bags on fire. That got really hectic. I remember Cowboy got a little singed 'cause he had a nylon sleeping bag and he couldn't get out of it quick enough. But the rest of us just cleared out.

My boyfriend, Mark, got picked up for previous warrants and went to gaol for six months. Halfway through his sentence he found out he had cancer. So he went into his chemotherapy through the gaol hospital. He was still receiving therapy when he got out and together we stayed outside St Canice's church in the middle of winter.

I had to train myself to wake up before Mark did because he was so ill at the time from the chemo and I knew the first thing that he would do [when he woke] was throw up. Within two or three weeks of him getting out of gaol we bought a car off a couple of backpackers. They wanted $800, but we got them down to $300. That sort of saved his life. Once he woke and was throwing up, he'd crawl down the steps [of the church] into the car. Then we'd drive down to the methadone clinic—I was on the treatment at the time—and we'd drive down to the park at Rushcutters Bay, have a coffee and joint, and think about the day. Then we'd go down to the hospital for his appointments. It was a hard, cold, dark winter.

The only thing and the best thing about [that time] was that it got me to get off heroin. It was this: either have Mark and no heroin so I could look after him, or have heroin and not have Mark. It was no contest. I'd met Mark five years before; he was a drug dealer in the Cross. He was getting mugged at the time I met him and I jumped in to help. We were friends after that and then I fell in love with him.

We got the [flat we're now living in] the day after he finished his treatment. We'd been put on a priority housing list after we got letters from the churches and the doctors' certificates, and we got the place within three months—but only because we pushed for it. If we didn't have the letters and the support we had, it would have been a lot harder. For people who aren't necessarily aware of what is available, it's so hard for them and they don't know what to do. [The authorities] don't help you do anything; you've got to find it yourself. Like, we needed counsellors, the clinic and all sorts of other stuff.

About six months after [we moved in to our place] we were told that the treatment was only half-successful. Apparently he [Mark] had two forms [of cancer], aggressive and non-aggressive. The chemo got rid of the aggressive. So, at the beginning of this year he had another treatment that wasn't as devastating, but he was still pretty sick. Then three weeks ago he was given the all-clear. If it comes back, considering how debilitating it was, we ain't doing the treatment again.

We've been in a stable environment for the last few years now and I started getting bored. My mind was dulled; I needed to use it. Because even while I was on the streets I was always doing my art-work. So I've started Year 10 at school, just to get back into study-ing again. Then I'm thinking of doing drug and alcohol studies. I've got no idea yet what I'll do with it, I just know I don't want to waste all those years of experience.

I've got to admit there are some really, really nice people that are willing to help [the homeless], but the majority of society ignores you completely—'We don't see you.' Or they go out of their way to be neg-ative. At the church I'm working at, I'm part of the church staff, and the attitude of some of the parishioners is so hypocritical compared to how it was when I lived on the steps outside the church. I was 'a thing'; now I'm a citizen. I haven't changed as a person; I've just got somewhere to live. I've had a real hard time dealing with that.

[The government departments] were very cooperative when they found out you were homeless, but not so cooperative when they found out you were a homeless drug addict. I think it's a case of, 'Drug addict? Too hard basket, don't worry about it.' Especially if you're a chronic drug addict, then it's 'Oh, she's never going to change.'

I found it was more so when I wanted to get off [the addiction]. The heroin itself is not a problem to get off, although the habit is. I needed to go onto the methadone when Mark was getting his chemo, and I went up the clinic. They were quite willing for me to go onto it. Every time I went in there they were encouraging me to go higher, higher and higher, but I stayed on the original dosage.

But then, when I'd been on it [the program] for twelve months and I wanted to come off it, they made so many excuses and made it so hard. I'd have to give regular urine [samples], have to see the doctor every time I wanted to come down. A lot of the clinics get paid for the [number of] people that go on it [the program], and they can let you go up to hundreds of mils [milligrams] of methadone. That's what I kept pointing out to them; the whole idea is that you want to get off it.

I can't understand it where you have a person with a six-month habit of heroin and twelve years later they're still on their methadone; they don't encourage you to quit. I am so glad I'm finished my treatment because it took me three months to recover. If I had of known [what it was going to be like], I would've gone cold turkey.

The hardest part of it all was if I had to be sleeping out anywhere by myself. Even if I was on the street I'd at least have one male with me for safety. I'm a big girl and I can handle myself, but there's no way I'd put myself in that situation again. Bad things do happen [to women on the street]. Some [female] friends of mine suffered worse; they ended up stuffed into sports bags and dumped in the river.

There was once a guy [around the Cross] and he was offering girls $200 for their hair. They've got an 'Ugly Mugs' thing where girls report [men like him] and the girls keep an eye out. But working girls don't go to the cops over rape charges because [the police know] you're a working girl or you're a [drug] user [or both], so the cops aren't going to help none of them.

From my perspective on homelessness, one of the things they need to do is admit there's females on the streets. [They need to] admit there are homeless women because there's not enough beds. We don't exist and it's hard to get resources when you don't exist. Women are supposed to stay at friends' places or they've got the streets. It's like we should be at home and we should have men who look after us. It's so hard to deal with that kind of attitude.

I mean, I've given up on social workers that talk to me, because you can tell within five minutes whether they understand the problem or whether they've done a degree and think they know the problem. It's like having a DOCS [Department of Community Services] worker who's twenty-one and never had a kid and telling you how you should do it!

We've got to admit there are problems; don't just walk over somebody that's in the gutter. Instead of just saying to your local council, 'Get them off the street, we don't like seeing them', there's got to be a change of attitude. And how do we change people's attitude towards the homeless? I still don't know.

Sallie

They need more initiatives. A counsellor from the Kirketon Road Centre did a drug talk one time and she asked me if I could talk to this politician. He asked me for ideas and I took him down the Cross and showed him all the places where people shoot up in the lanes and the alleyways with all the fits [syringes] on the ground. The next day we got the shooting gallery in the Cross.

So you can change politicians, but so many people don't want to try. And also, a lot of people don't want changes for some reason, not so much the public—more the 'haves' than the 'have-nots'. Especially in the Cross, because the gap [between the 'haves' and the 'have-nots'] is so extreme there. It was the same with Rough Edges [Drop-in Centre]. When they first opened their doors it was just the Rough Edges coordinator, one of ministers from the church [St John's] and me working in shifts. That was until they started getting volunteers working there. But they've been having opposition [to their being there] since they first opened.

So many people [in power] make decisions about what is necessary based on what they think; they don't actually ask anyone what they need or what they want. You'll find out that fixing the problem would be easier if you actually made it easier to get the resources that are available. Ask them [the homeless] what they want. Cut the red tape in half, at the very least.

If you've got trouble with reading and writing and you've got to go through half a dozen forms to get to the resources, you ain't going to do it. Even though Mark and I are quite smart people, there was [still] so much paperwork to do. I don't know about those that aren't quite as smart; it's no wonder they're still on the street with the red tape they have to get through.

Sallie

For me, over the next couple years, I just want to be here [where I am in life now]. I want to continue broadening my mind and enjoying the time me and Mark have got left. I still want to talk to my real dad, but my mum passed away four years ago. Mum denied my stepdad abused us up until the day she died. But karma's got my stepdad because these days he's a barfly—I didn't have to do a thing. But it troubled me for a long time, and one of the reasons why I did use drugs was to numb it all. With St Canice's they do regular retreats for senior students in Catholic schools for their social justice studies. I did talks there about my experiences, and with these talks, and over the last few years or so, I've felt it's [become] easier for me.

And I know I've made a 180-degree turn. I went into the church [St Canice's] a couple of weeks ago and the wind was so cold. It was so cold it reminded me of how cold it would be at night when I was sleeping there, and I'll never let it happen again.

Tom 'Animal' Lee
age 55

I got the nickname 'Animal' years ago when I was in a band. I was the drummer, although I used to love playin' the electric guitar. There was a group of us and we all picked the name of someone out of *The Muppet Show*. Someone said, 'You're Animal' [the drummer]. So I said, 'Fair enough.'

I grew up out at Fairfield in Sydney with me two brothers and parents. We had a normal family, whatever normal is, like every other kid; Mum and Dad workin' and we'd just entertain ourselves until Mum and Dad came home in the afternoon. Mum and Dad would get up early [to go to work] and we'd let ourselves out and let ourselves back in, in the afternoon. They used to call us 'latch-key kids'. We didn't mind; it'd give us more time to play outside.

That's what it was like in them days. Everyone had little gangs and we all belonged to a gang. Every weekend this gang would fight that gang, and then that gang would fight this gang—just harmless punch-ups. None of these knives [like today], you know, no kickin', no nothin'. That was one of the laws, our laws—no kickin', no sticks, no stones. Just fists. Clean fightin'.

When I was sixteen I left home to become a jockey down in Randwick. Well, I was scared of horses, but me dad said, 'I can't afford to keep sendin' yeh to school.' They had to pay school fees and buy textbooks and all that and Mum and Dad couldn't afford it. So he says, 'Well I got yeh a job. You're goin' to be a jockey.' So I said, 'What's a jockey?' He [just] said they ride horses at the races. I thought, well I'd like to have a look at it.

I loved it straight off the bat. The first time I went on it I thought, here's this bloody big horse and I'm just this little kid! But I thought I'd give it a go and the trainer said to me, 'Yeah, no worries. Move in.' 'Course I had to live in the stables down where the horses were. I had to clean their boxes out at three o'clock in the mornin' before breakfast! Horse shit, first thing in the morning! Beautiful! I did jockeying for about three and a half years. [Then] I had a fall. The horse on the other side fell and I went over the top and got kicked around the head a bit. That put me out of action for about twelve months and they [the stables] said, 'Don't come back.'

Well I [knew] I didn't want to go home. So, at eighteen or so, I saw an ad in the paper for the civil service. I sat the exam and got it. I was in the Tax Office. I was popular because I knew all about racin' and they were all mad punters. Then, when I was nineteen and a half I got called up for National Service in 1969 [and] I did me two years [of service]. Vietnam was still on. So away I went. I got me hat on, they gave me this bloody rifle and I know what the pointy end does—that's the way it was. It was alright because I was stationed at Saigon. You'd go to work and take a bottle of scotch with you. You know, we made the best of it.

I got engaged before I went over. Me father-in-law thought if somethin' happened to me I'd get somethin' [monetary] out of the government. That's what he thought! He even told me! I thought, I'm goin' to love being related to you! [He was] lookin' at me like I was a goldmine! I came back [from Vietnam] and got married in 1970—not a bad way to spend four weeks of leave.

[Back in Vietnam] I went out on one patrol. Twelve of us went out and six of us came back. I was in Signals [and] I had to go out because their regular Signalman was sick or something and they said, 'You haven't been out on patrol yet, have you? Grab your radio pack. Go on!' They, the radio packs, were about ten kilos and you had a little bloke like me carryin' it. I called another bloke over who was bigger [than me] and said, 'You carry it.' When I had to use it, it was like, 'Stand still for a minute will yeh, so I can call!'

When I got back [to Australia] I settled down [with my wife] and bought a house. Everyone reckoned when I came back I was different. 'You're fuckin' different.' That's what everyone used to say to me. I felt the same as I always was, but after a while I was keeping in contact with all the guys I'd been over there with. We'd meet all the time, every weekend. We'd all sit around and say to each other, 'Are you being treated differently?' We thought we were all mad, like, 'Have we got a disease or something?' There were no counsellors then; the word 'counselling' never even came up. So we just had each other. It was isolation.

Tom 'Animal' Lee

[When] I came back, the Tax Office held me job open for me but I left it. I couldn't handle it. They treated me like I did have some sort of disease. I got called a 'pig' and a 'bastard' [but] none of them got called up. You did your army service or you went to gaol for twelve months—that was the choice. Twelve months drinking scotch and a job when I got back or twelve months in gaol? I didn't want to go to gaol.

But I wasn't aware of what I was gettin' into. I just wasn't. If you listened to the news [about the war] all you heard was the bad stuff, but I ignored it. When you were there it's not like you could say, 'I've had enough of this. I don't want to play any more', then jump on a plane and go home. You can't do that.

I couldn't understand it [the treatment from people]. Like I said, there was no-one back then you could go to for help. You'd go and see your own doctor and he'd say, 'Never mind. It'll be right. Here, take some Valium.' There was no-one trained in that area. 'It'll go away,' he'd say, 'take some more Valium or Seropax. Have a couple of beers.'

We really didn't know what to do so we tended to stick together and smoked dope and drank beers on the weekend. You know [it was like], 'What did yeh do on the weekend?' You'd go, 'Don't know, but it must have been good.' You couldn't remember.

[There were] five guys that I went away [to Vietnam] with and I'm the last one of them left. A couple committed suicide. A couple died ... gave up and whatever. And now [that] I'm living homeless I think, shit, when am I going to go? Sometimes I wish it would happen real quick and other days ... nah. [It's] up and down.

After I got out [of the army] in 1971 I chucked in the Tax Office job after three months and went into a different field altogether—

in insurance. I did that for fifteen years, handling workers' comp [compensation] claims. Most of them were serious claims then and most insurance companies would settle. You'd go to court for a couple of hours then have a couple of scotches at lunchtime, drinking with solicitors and judges.

During that time I was livin' out at Windsor [with my wife]. We had a girl and a boy. [They were] beautiful. [Then] we split up in the late 1970s–early 1980s when my daughter was about ten and my son was eight and a half. It just wasn't workin'. We'd known each other for years but we just couldn't live with each other any more. We sat down one night and said, 'This isn't workin' out any more, is it?' 'Nah. How about we have a couple of drinks on it?' So we had a couple of drinks and just decided—that's it. Told the kids in the morning. Dad's moving out. See you later, Dad. I gave her [my wife] the house—well, she was going to keep the kids. I found a flat.

I won a bit a money on the horses then I met another woman and was livin' out at Richmond—new woman, new job. I left the insurance job [and] got a job in transport with Steggles Chickens. One day they called me in off the floor [offering me the job of] Assistant Transport Officer or something. It had to do with computers, which I knew about. I thought I'd give it a go. Me manager lasted about twelve months and I got his job. He didn't know as much about the [computer] system as I did. Got himself sacked [as a result].

I'd streamlined the whole [computer] system for him. It managed twenty-two trucks and I enjoyed it. Good thing about [the job was] I could start whenever I wanted and finish whenever I wanted.

Soon as the trucks got back, bang! Go home, bang! Down to the pub. I'd knock off at two o'clock [in the afternoon]. I'd start at five o'clock in the morning. There's no-one around to hassle you [that early], so I just stuck straight into it. I'd have eighty per cent of my work done before anyone else got to work. In 1996 they sold out to Inghams and that was that. They offered redundancies. I took me money; it was better than nothin'.

Then I came home one day from the pub and found me missus in bed with another bloke. I thought, this is good! This is me best mate! I just walked out, went to the pub, and me other mates at the pub said, 'You've just found out, haven't yeh?' They knew about it. I asked them, 'How long was this goin' on for?' They said six months. They said, 'You didn't do anything, did yeh?' 'Nah,' I said.

So that was 1996. Chucked the job in and hit the booze real bad. I said [to the company], 'Give me my money, I'm outta here.' I thought, ah, what the fuck? What else can the world do to me? Kick me in the gut a few times? I went down the park and played 'pass the flagon [of booze]'. I virtually did nothin'. I was livin' with one of me mates. He was workin', I was drinkin'. I realised it at the time [that I was an alcoholic]. You know you're an alcoholic when you can't get up in the mornin' and you can't even have your Weetbix until you've had two schooners. I was always a heavy drinker. But when I was in the army there was nothin' else to do. So you'd go down the pub, you know.

They put me on a disability pension with me alcoholism and I went into rehab. I had to go see the government doctor [and] prove I was an alcoholic. That was easy. I just walked in there normal. I came straight from the pub and he said, 'Jesus! How many 'ave you 'ad?' I said, 'I don't know, I don't count any more.' The doctor stamped the form and said, 'Go on! Piss off! You're an alcoholic.' I was only in there five minutes! That was it. I wouldn't suggest to anybody to get on it [the disability pension for alcoholism] because it just doesn't work. There are follow-up tests and once every four or eight months or whatever they send you this letter [looking] for a doctor's report. Now, you tell me a doctor that can treat alcoholism! Maybe the publican can fill [the report] out for me 'cause I visit him regularly. He'd know more; he dispenses me medicine. He gets rid of the shakes.

You find out [that you're an alcoholic when] you start to lose all those people you used to call friends. You might have ten to start off with that you'd call close friends and then after a few months or whatever there's just five and then there's two and then it's just you and the drink. Then you realise, ah shit! What have I done bloody wrong? Ah, fuck 'em anyway. What am I going to go back to them [me mates] for anyway? They're just going to turn away as soon as something goes wrong again. I wasn't bothered puttin' the effort into moving on. You find yourself not happy, but comfortable in that position.

So, I just asked around what was the hardest [rehab] program to be in. I heard 'The Sally's' [The Salvation Army]. Took me eighteen months to do a ten-month program! When you come out, you graduate. 'Woo-hoo! I graduated! No more alcoholic!' I got $100 [at the end]. I hadn't had a drink in ten months so I went straight to the pub! Back where I started. Two months later I went back and did the relapse program. It was good. I enjoyed it.

Tom 'Animal' Lee

There were also guys who were comin' off drugs as well. Shit, I thought I had problems! Some of them had something happen to them as kids. That gave me a bit more belief in meself, a bit more courage to go on. You know, all the shit he's been through and he's come out. If he can do it, I can do it. It was an eye-opener. This is what life is really about. This is the other side people don't even know about, even the politicians going, 'Ah, it doesn't happen', or like prostitution, 'It's not on the Cross.' Nah, it's the girls just talkin' up there; it's their social club! They meet every night to see who can wear the most make-up!

Anyway, the first two weeks [in rehab] is difficult. As soon as you walk in them doors you pay $110 up front and that's it; the doors are closed. You're not allowed out [if you want to stay in the program]. Four weeks locked up. If you want smokes you've got to send someone out to the shop. Two blokes walked out and I was nearly one of them. I stepped up to the front door a couple of times. You can walk out anytime.

It wasn't supposed to be religious-based [but] it was heavily religious-based. They said they did talk about God and Jesus but they wouldn't force it on you. That was completely opposite to the way it actually was. 'You will go to church on Tuesday. You will go to church on Thursday. You will go to church on Sunday. And if you don't, you get out of the program.' It's really heavy.

What happens if I don't believe in God? You can't say you're not going to church. You've got to or otherwise you're out the door. They still do this as far as I know. But they look at it as though, if one bloke walks out there'd be another bloke to take his place. It's a big money spinner for them. You've got to pay to go into it and they take eighty per cent of your welfare benefit as well. It's just making money off unfortunate people. Then they go to the government saying they need more funding for the alcohol program.

But I think in my own case, it certainly saved my life. I reckon I would have been dead by now. I'm still drinking but I've got some control over it. I haven't got complete control, but if I hadn't done the [Salvation Army] program I might have been dead. I think that I found a peace with meself in it. It's like I'm not such a bad bastard after all as everyone was saying. I started to believe it after being fairly hard on meself. It's some sort of happiness with meself. I'm starting to like meself a bit. I found a happy medium— if you don't like me it's your problem, not mine. Not everybody's got to like me. There's good and bad in everybody. But you know, that's life.

After I came out [of rehab] the second time I lived at Foster House [men's shelter] for about eighteen months. I had a single room and a colour TV. That cost $96 a week and that included your meals. I was still on the pension, the disability pension. Then I had a flat out at Mascot with a mate. I'd known him in the war. It was alright for a while [but then I] couldn't handle him any more. He didn't know how to cook and I was doin' all the cookin' all the time. I had to chase him up all the time for the rent and food money. So I chucked it in, and mainly ever since then I've been livin' on the streets. I've been on the streets for about two years now.

The first time [I slept on the street] was fairly scary. I didn't sleep much at all. [It was] up in Hyde Park, under one of the benches with some newspapers over the top of me. That was in autumn.

I thought, shit, what am I doing here? What's the next thing that's going to happen to me? The cops came through with a police dog, a big German Shepherd lookin' at me. I was thinking, piss off dog!

They try and move you on: 'On you go.' I said, 'Where am I going to go?' They don't care, so you're walking up and down the streets all night. There's no-one in the park at that time of night except for homeless people [but] they'd rather see you walking up and down the streets instead of sleeping in the park. It's a people's park, that's what I always thought. But you'd end up going back about half an hour later [to sleep] under the same bench. They're just making sure we don't steal each other's drugs!

[In the end] I thought, I'm not sleeping in the park any more, I'm not going to get any sleep tonight. I ended up having to arm myself with a knife. Had to. You didn't know. How hopeless did I look? I thought, fuck this. There's got to be a different side to life.

One day, I was drinking in a pub near Central [station] at eight in the morning and this guy said, 'What's the time, mate? I got to make a phone call at nine o'clock. I got to ring up Homeless Persons and find out where I'm sleeping tonight.' I'd never heard of them. I rang them up. They said, 'Yeah, you can stay with us. Six o'clock.' 'How much?' I asked. 'Nothin'.' A couple of times I rang up and they were all full and I ended up sleepin' in the park with me neighbours playin' that pastor game again—'pastor flagon'. You know, pass the flagon.

So you ring up at nine every morning or six at night. At nine you usually have a place by quarter past. If you miss out—some are not available in the morning—you ring up at six that night. You adapt to it. You do it the first couple of times and you don't feel real good about yourself. But it then becomes second nature to you; there's not much choice. Second nature for me is to go straight to a phone box every morning. If I've got no money I reverse the charges. You can usually get somewhere. Just give your name and your birth date.

Some of the places you do the washing up after dinner. That goes a long way 'cause they're only volunteers. So you wash up and wipe for them. Sometimes you can stay in during the day and watch videos. It's better than sittin' in the park or the pub all day.

There are some [shelters] you go to that are a dormitory-type situation. You've got to sleep with one eye open and your wallet in your pillowcase it's that bad. You don't know who is [sleeping there]. A lot of them are alcoholics or drug addicts and they're all hanging out for a beer or drugs or whatever and [will use] any means to get it. I found what I try to do is stick with alcoholics. An alcoholic will share his last drink with yeh. A drug addict will knock you over the head and grab your wallet, even if he's your mate. It's a chemical thing. I haven't got much against them. I know they've got an addiction as much as I have.

A lot [of homeless people] sleep out in summer. Coming towards winter—that's when it gets hard. That's why rehab gets bigger numbers in the winter. Guaranteed increase, autumn through winter. As soon as summer's here, even if you're halfway through a rehab program, a lot of guys throw themselves out [of rehab]. 'So long. I'm off. Thanks for the accommodation. See you next winter!' [In summer] I sleep indoors. It's too hard. A dog'll piss on you or cop'll kick you in the guts [and say] 'Get up yeh mongrel.' They're generally pretty good ... but you get the odd ones, no matter where you go.

Tom 'Animal' Lee

Now and again [in the shelters] there'll be some idiot who wants to fight. As soon as that happens, whoever started it gets thrown out. If they're not sure which one started it, both get thrown out. They don't argue 'cause you're not going to argue with twenty blokes that are angry and want to get to sleep! It's a simple rule and the [volunteer] workers know it, so they feel safe.

When I first started [sleeping rough] no-one knew. That's when I was sleeping in a park in Richmond in the old bandstand. We knew how to get into a storeroom out the back that nobody ever used—me and another bloke. It was a case of necessity and it was open.

For getting something to eat there's the food vans around the city. You could go for six weeks without having to buy food, easy. All you've got to get used to is the taste of the food. Some [food vans] are not so good. You go, 'That one's good, that's one's not as good, [like a restaurant] that's four stars, no stars, that one's not that bad!' But you're getting a feed, and that's what's important. All these meal vans—I don't where they get their money but it's obvious they don't get much.

Since I've been homeless I'm not in contact with me old mates. Completely cut off. I don't worry about it—that's the past; get on with the future. It's the same with me family. Me daughter and me son, I haven't seen them for years. I traced me daughter last July to let her know that her grandfather died but I'm not in contact with them now. It was hard [when my father died]. I had to go up to Port Macquarie and had to organise the funeral and pay for it. Me little brother lives up in the top end of Queensland. So I tracked him down and he said, 'Well I don't have any money.' I said, 'I don't want any money. I'm just lettin' you know Dad died.' So he said,

'If you don't need any money I'll come down for the funeral, just tell us when it is.'

Mum died when I was eighteen. She passed out at work and that was it. Me middle brother, Bobby, died. He committed suicide about eight years ago. I had to go up and plant him as well. All I seem to be doing is planting me family! I planted Mum, I planted me dad, I planted me brother. I've only got one left. I [jokingly] keep ringing him up saying, 'Watch out! You're next on the list.'

[With Bobby] I don't know [what happened]. When I rang up to find out, I learned he had two girlfriends up there, they'd lived with him, but I couldn't track them down. He never left a [suicide] note or anything like that. He'd been dead in bed for about three days when they found him. I had to go up and clean it out and get rid of all his stuff. I just brought it around to The Sally's [The Salvation Army] and told them to take the lot. They'll come around if there's something for free. I hadn't even got him in the ground yet and they were around! But there was nothing I wanted.

So I had to fork it out [funeral expenses] for me brother and me dad. I found out [my dad] had about $600 or $700 in a bank account no-one knew he had, and stuffed [some] down the back of a cupboard or something. So I had to prove who I was and got that out and then I had to pay it straight to the funeral director. He let me off without paying about $1600. He said, 'Matey, don't worry.' Well I didn't have all the money for it so what am I going to do? Put him half in the ground? Or half-bury him? I know, dig half a hole with his legs hangin' out! Or we could just have half the ceremony; Our Father I only half-liked him anyway! What are you going to do?

Tom 'Animal' Lee

Me daughter and me son don't like me much any more because I haven't got any money. I had a great relationship [with them] and me ex-wife when I was working. I used to earn $60,000 or $70,000 a year, so I was never short a quid. It was always, 'Hey Dad, can you spare me a couple of hundred?' Then later it was like, 'Hey Dad, you haven't got a job any more. We'll see you around.' That pissed me right off; I was very angry. I thought, what have I done wrong? I had a great relationship with me kids when I had money. That was the last thing I said to my daughter: 'Well I still love you.' She didn't say anything. I hung up.

Over time I've stayed at a couple of places where you're allowed to stay for three months, then they piss you off. They put a note under your door saying your three months is up and that you have to vacate the room by ten o'clock, and then tell you the date. Fair enough. You pay your money, $100 a week or whatever. It's hard [paying for accommodation], especially when you're on a pension.

At the moment a young lady [at The Station Drop-in Centre] is working on getting me an independent house. If you want help like that, The Station is one of the best places to get it. They treat you like a person. Some places treat you like you're a kid, almost like it's all your fault that you're like that. You're a naughty boy. Sit down. Eat that. If you don't like it, get out. They may as well kick you in the gut.

[But] not many of them think like that. Some of them have different activities. There are people who can help you with housing or people in different medical fields that are genuinely there to help you if you want it, but you've got to ask for it. They'll help you as much as possible. [However, some places with accommodation] treat you as a little number. But there's nothing in those three months to really motivate you. [I think] they need to give [homeless people] a purpose—development programs. There are good programs that might help you find what you're looking for by way of permanent housing or something like that.

There's art and crafts you can do. But a lot of them don't do that. [Sometimes] you go to sign up for a course and you go, 'What's this?' They'll say, 'Don't worry about applying for that because it's not going to happen next week.' They [would have] just put it up on the board. I've seen that a couple of times and I think, if you knew it wasn't going to happen why put it up on the notice board?

In some [fee-based temporary accommodation] places if you ask a question, or too many questions, you'll be [kicked] out within a week. And you're paying for the service! It's go there, pay your rent, shut up, eat, sleep, wake up, or get out because [the place closes] for the day or whatever. Just pay your rent. It's not open [for discussion]. It's their rules and that's it. [People] have no choice, they just go, 'That's the rules, I'll play by them.'

In the end you just say, 'Oh, alright.' You just give up on trying to be yourself and trying to be independent about the decisions that affect your life. I don't bother arguing any more or asking them questions. You're just like a puppet. You just feel like you're losing your own identity. You're not a real person. You just walk around, and that's it. [You] don't know how you're going to fill in the day. You lose track of what day it is. In some of the places if you know they've got an art class on Monday and this on a Wednesday and that on a Thursday, it helps you start to feel good about yourself. I think that's what's missing in a lot of places.

Tom 'Animal' Lee

I don't go to The Station [Drop-in Centre] on Saturdays and Sundays because it's not open, but there are other places that are. I look forward to Mondays so I can get back to The Station because there are people [there] I know I can talk to, and they listen. They genuinely care for you if you want to care for yourself. To me, that really makes me feel good about myself.

There were times I've thought about killing meself. I've spoken to a few other guys and it's the same thing. So I've thought about it, but I go, 'Nah, nah, nah.' I haven't got the guts to kill myself. I tried it once. It was about eight years ago. I don't really remember why [I decided to try it]. I just got pissed. Apparently I said to one of the guys, 'I've had enough, I'm going to kill myself.' It was a blur. I just fell down on the ground and thought, nothing good is gonna ever happen to me again. All I know is I woke up and I was band-aged [along both forearms].

They [the hospital] said they were transferring me. I said, 'Oh! Where am I going to?' They said, 'Never you mind.' They sent me to Cumberland [Hospital] psychiatric ward. I didn't know where I was, nobody told me. I thought, hang on, there's a lot of loonies in here. I was wondering how come they were talking to me like I was a four-year-old kid or something. It was terrifying. I sat down play-ing their game for about four or five hours until I finally got to see the shrink. We had a cup of coffee. He asked me, 'What would you like to do now?' I said, 'I'd like to go and have a fuckin' beer, mate.' He said, 'Well. You go out that front door, the gate's up there. There's a security guard up there. Just wave to him and tell him you're just going up to the pub for a beer. Be back here by six

suburb of Punchbowl. It was a War Service home for returned servicemen. I lived there for about twenty-five years. Even though I was registered for school I don't think I did more than a month [in total] in fifteen years at school because of my ill health. I'm now getting a chance to get the education that I missed out on.

In May 1956 I went into the book industry, where I worked for nearly thirty years, until the recession of the early 1980s. I worked in sales and book ordering, working in various bookshops. During all that time I had relationships with women. I was even engaged twice, once for three years. In the 1960s I started to feel different. People started to say that I was more masculine–feminine than feminine–masculine. I was a female in a male's body. I felt I was far more interested in getting involved with women's backgrounds rather than men's.

I did parachute jumps for my recovery with asthma. [That was after] I had my left lung removed in 1974. Since then I haven't had an asthma attack. [Back then] I also did competitive and theatrical [sword] fencing. The theatrical fencing was on the theatrical stage at talent quests and duelling exhibitions. In competitive fencing I never won the Australian Championship, but I held the NSW sword fencing title three years running in the mid-1970s.

Then around the early 1980s I had a problem with a genie—the type that comes out of a bottle—alcohol. Some people call it 'lunatic soup'. My problem with alcohol came from loneliness and not getting support or acceptance from people as a result of my gender condition; I was losing my self-esteem.

Through my alcoholism I ended up with sclerosis of the liver and brain damage. I spent a lot of time in mental health institutions around Sydney. As a blood donor I had given a large amount of donations. But because I had sclerosis they couldn't take any more blood from me.

In the 1980s I legally changed my name, but I kept my surname. By 1985 the [NSW] Department of Housing and Social Security officially recognised that I used to be David Lyall Richard Coad, but was now Davina Lesley Robyn Coad [in] my new lifestyle.

Then, in 1985, I was mutilated by two men. They weren't picked up for what they did to me, but in 1986 they were involved in a murder which I prefer not to discuss. For that other crime, the murder, they were put away, never to be released. In 1985, I started undergoing the surgical procedures for a gender reassignment. I went to doctors, psychiatrists and plastic surgeons. I had three operations but the surgery wasn't working. Finally, on 22 August 1988 I went through with the gender reassignment surgery.

In 1993 I did something illegal and got a little bit of a holiday for it in a centre for women—a women's prison. Because of my new lifestyle I had no problems there.

When I lived in [the Sydney suburb of] Mosman in the early 1990s I was under the Department of Housing, but was evicted. At that time I was due to go into rehab at Rozelle, but they couldn't help my alcoholism. So when I left there I didn't have anywhere to go. That was in 1995. I started making applications with the YWCA [NSW] for accommodation, but they said no. I looked everywhere I could. That's when my homelessness problem began. I stayed in a few homeless shelters for short periods. I also lived in parks, like Hyde Park, and in trains and public toilets, wherever I could. It wasn't very nice.

A counsellor at the Kirketon Road Centre [in Darlinghurst] took me down to the Department of Housing and they put me on the housing list. A couple of years after that they finally found me a place. That's where I've been staying since.

I'm still going to Alcoholics Anonymous meetings. [Right now] I have been ten months sober. I'm trying not to become homeless again or touch the lunatic soup and trying to work on my recovery. I've done it my way and it may not be the 'correct' way, but I'm using my [recovery] time to work with other people [alcoholics and the homeless]. I've also been involved with community [welfare and religious] organisations that have helped support me with my alcoholism, too.

When I was homeless it was very difficult for me because there were more places for men than for women [in homeless shelters]. The other problem is that they'd also say, 'If we put you in with women, would women accept you?' It was very hard. And they couldn't send me down to Edward Eager Lodge [in Darlinghurst] or Matthew Talbot [Hostel in Woolloomooloo] either. It's a problem if you're a member of the genderless society. There is a place for transgender, called Teresa House, but it's only for certain situations. It's also a problem if you have, as I do, a borderline personality disorder.

The worst part for me is [trying] to be accepted by people. Some people say they will accept me, but they don't. Of course I'm only speaking of myself, my situation. Unfortunately, even though I had a family in the background, they couldn't accept my new lifestyle either. They said they could understand the problem but just couldn't get involved. It has meant that I had to leave a lot of things [in my life] because they couldn't accept 'Davina'.

All I know is that I want to be part of the community and to not quit. They do say, 'The first step of failure is the first step of success.' And I don't want to be served; I want to serve the community. You have to keep trusting and keep believing. For me, I won't give up because that's the first part of being homeless again, the first part of having no fixed address.

For society to deal with homelessness, firstly I think there needs to be more publicity on it. Everyone is an individual and everyone should have a say, which they don't. We should not treat people as a number; treat them as a person.

I'm not educated, but all I know is I try to be an apostle, to be a witness and to help people. Action does speak louder than words so I do a lot of volunteer work, such as talking to people like those at the Vincentian Village [homeless drop-in centre in Darlinghurst]. I've been helping the office of the Lord Mayor [of Sydney] and I donate to the Wesley Mission. I believe immortality is living a life worth remembering, and Davina does not want to end up as a loser.

[Due to my mental illness] and because they reckoned my lifestyle had become unmanageable, I was put under two orders, a Public Guardian Order[3], which is managed under the Office of the NSW Protective Commissioner. I'm currently under the guardianship of Our Lady Nurses of the Poor, or the Brown Nurses, and the Department of Housing. Just recently, they've threatened to pull my life support with the Public Guardian Order. I'm not against the organisations, of course; I'm only talking about particular personalities within it.

I was told [by the organisations that] I'm not communicating or cooperating with them. They say, 'Your living lifestyle is not up to scratch.' They reckon that my abode has become unmanageable. I've brought this to the attention of the Department of Housing. If things go badly I will then have no fixed address; there's a possibility I'll be homeless again.

To me, I don't need a Public Guardian Order because I think I'm working on myself, making decisions for myself and taking responsibility for myself. It's not up to the Brown Nurses or the Department of Housing to do it. I am responsible and I decide. All I'm asking them for is this: yes, we know there is a problem—I'm asking for time to solve that problem. I'm not sure what will happen.

For me, working on my sobriety comes first. I have a very selfish motive, my recovery from alcoholism. Before, I was homeless. At the moment, I'm at the risk of being homeless. Maybe the final result is that I will be homeless.

A lot of things happened to me at the beginning of this year. I've lost twenty-five kilograms in three months, which I'm addressing at the moment. My mind and my body are in two different places, so it's hard going. But I'm not going to quit or go back into alcohol and I'm definitely not going to commit suicide. And as someone once told me, 'Davina, you're like a tea bag; you don't know your full strength until you get into hot water.'

Since the interview, Davina's situation has improved. The disagree-

Davina Coad

ments with the Brown Nurses have been resolved amicably for both sides and she now has permanent accommodation. Davina has stayed sober for over a year and her health is improving. Throughout it all, she has continued her voluntary work in the homeless community.

Ray Sippel
age 53

I was born in Quirindi, in NSW. I moved to Tamworth when I was five years old with me three sisters. I'm only talking to one [sister] at the present. I had me first job when I was fourteen, cutting chooks' necks for nine months. Then I went and did spot-welding for seven years, making poultry cages. I left there when I was twenty and went to Golden Circle Canneries in Brisbane for twelve months. After that I went to Perth and was crushing manganese for eighteen months.

Finally, after spending four years in New Zealand, I came back to Sydney in 1980, ran out of money and just started living on the streets. I was trying to find work, but there was none. There was the recession and the bloody unions wouldn't allow you to work unless you had a ticket. I'd go up north doing fruit-picking, earn a bit of money, then come back to Sydney and blow it and be back on the streets. I still went fruit-picking and followed the seasons around. [I went to] Young picking cherries; Shepparton picking pears; Orange picking apples. [Always] back to Sydney and back on the streets.

In Sydney [when I was first sleeping rough] I met a couple of [homeless] old blokes and I met Colin, who showed me the ropes for a couple of years. He's still sleeping out [on the street] after forty years—he's seventy-three. He sleeps up at Central [Station] in the doorways.

It wakes you up a bit [being homeless]. You've got to fight for everything you get. Everything I have I carry in a big black carry bag. The first night I spent on the streets was in Hyde Park, that's when Colin walked past and seen me sleeping there and told me where to go for the next night. So I slept down at Circular Quay for six months on public seats and in bus shelters.

When the Matthew Talbot [Hostel] was full they used to put mattresses down on the floor after eleven o'clock. When they stopped that I started sleeping out all year round. I still used the Talbot for meeting people, washing and showering. You don't have to walk around the city dirty. You don't have to be a grub. Some people, if you washed them, it'd kill 'em! The dirt is what is keeping them alive. The dirt helps to keep all their pores closed so they don't feel the cold.

In 1988 I went back to Quirindi for four years to look after me grandmother until she died in 1992. I was on a carer's pension and she gave me a roof over me head while I looked after her and cooked for her. When she died, the [family] cleaned the house out, a block of flats sit there now. She was buried on that Saturday and I was back on the streets in Sydney.

Ray Sippel

The streets have been hard. I've been in fights. Some [of the general public] are alright [to me]. Others hassle me a bit. I've had to defend meself. Years ago you could walk around not watching your back. These days there are too many junkies and young ones that hang around in gangs. They get a bit of Dutch courage, but if you get 'em one-on-one they run like mongrel dogs.

On Pitt Street, they used to have big TV screens in the window and there'd be about twenty fellas sitting around on [milk] crates in the night. I was there for about two years. Then one of the old fellas just kept on crapping down the stairs and the security guards said, 'That's it!' So we moved up to a little arcade and stayed there for about six months. The same thing kept happening, people pissin' all over the place. Then we went to Town Hall for a while and got chased out of there, too. Some [guys] were bugging people for money, coal-biters and that.

Coal-biters [are] people who beg for money on the street. They make it hard for the other homeless people. Most people think that everyone who is livin' on the streets is a coal-biter [but] we're not. Most of the coal-biters these days are junkies. They sit on the street, make eighty dollars and then go straight up the Cross and shoot up.

Eventually, I was living on a window ledge up where Pitt Street and George Street meet, at the old railway headquarters under the arches. There'd be two bodies on each ledge. Everyone [sleeping] there knew everyone else; we looked after each other. I remember I got hassled there one night. I had a blue coat [on] and I was laying with me hand tucked inside it. Me other hand was wrapped around the strap of me bag. I woke up suddenly and thought, how come I got three hands? There was this fella going into me pocket after me wallet! I said [to him], 'If I hit the concrete, you're bloody dead!' The ledge I used to sleep on was about a metre off the ground. He just pulled his hand out [of my pocket] and shot off around the corner. That was a Friday night [when] they all come in [from the suburbs] to let their hair down.

When I was living on the ledge I wasn't getting the dole. I used to live on phonecards and money I'd find in the street. I stayed there [living on the ledge] for about six years before a counsellor got me into the Matthew Talbot [Hostel]. She used to run the Outreach Program. Every week she'd come and give you a meal ticket. She got me onto the dole too. I stayed at Talbot for two months and I went into the Outreach Program, into one of the houses for seven months. You've got to have a bloody good story to get in there, though.

There's a lot of people sleeping in the lanes around the Talbot. The cops clean the lane out on the first Monday or so of every month, they come with a council truck. Everything [goes] in the back of the truck, blankets and mattresses. But the cops have been alright generally. When [my mate] George was sleeping up at Central [Station] the cops used to come. You couldn't lie down [to sleep] where the buses were until the last bus pulled out, after about ten-thirty [at night]. The cops would watch [as homeless people arrived to set up]. They'd go through the group saying, 'You're in, you're in, you're in. Oh, a new fella? What's your name?' They'd do a warrant check. They look out for you and sometimes have a chat with you.

Same with the security guards. On the ledges [where I was living] old Lenny, a security guard, used to come out in the winter months and give us coffee. [In turn] we'd watch outside [for him]. Most guards would let you stay anywhere as long as you pack your gear and keep it clean.

[After staying at the Talbot] I was at a Housing Commission place in Redfern. I stayed there for two years. I got jack of it. Every Sunday I'd go to the Talbot, sit down and see the boys [old mates] and they used to hassle me about jumping the [housing] queue. They'd been on the waiting list for years and I was [only] waiting for twelve months. Anyway, I got hassled too many times. I went home one Sunday and I thought, fuck it. I wrote a letter to the Housing Commission, stuck me keys under the door and walked out. I came back last year from some fruit-picking and found out that I owed them $1000 in rent. I've already paid $600 back; I still got $400 to pay.

It's amazing how many people sleep out here in Sydney. It would open up a lot of people's eyes. There are about thirty or forty people [sleeping] up around the [State] Library alone. About forty [people sleep] at the car park in York Street. Everyone has got their own little nook and cranny, a dark corner.

[Over the years] I've known a hell of a lot of people on the streets. Some I know by face. A couple I know by name, like George and Colin and a couple of others. We were all sticking in one group. You know, who's doing what. Who's robbing what. Who's shooting up.

There are even lawyers and doctors [living on the streets]. I don't know if he's still practising, but old Bruce used to be a lawyer until he got a gutful. I think he had a breakdown or something and left his practice. Up to about five years ago if you had a warrant or a bluey [cop] after you, you might see Bruce of a Wednesday up at Town Hall in the square there. He used to sit there [listen to your problem] and say, 'I can fix that.' He'd go to court for you. I haven't seen him [for a while].

There's about 100 000 homeless people in Australia. That includes families, too. Over the past few years I've seen families out on the streets—whole families; mothers, fathers, kids. They get help quicker than single folks. I saw one family up at Town Hall; just young parents and two kids huddled together. Put it this way, if you go past any bus shelter after midnight and see a family there, they're probably homeless. I've seen young families picked up by DOCS [Department of Community Services]. They come and take the kids off them [the parents] and put them in a shelter that night. The next morning they take them to court and get full authority to put them in a foster home.

Then there are young girls up in the Cross selling themselves for their pimps [that] might allow 'em [the girls] to keep $20 out of $100. Many are going on sixteen [years of age]. The cops pick the young ones up and try to get them home and put them in shelters for the night. All of the funny farms [mental health institutions] have been closed down. So [you can see] some of them [ex-patients] walking around like zombies.

There's a lot of talk and no fuckin' action [when it comes to solving homelessness]. They promise everything and just don't live up to their promises. The government should get off its bloody arse and get more money for the shelters. If a shelter only has enough beds for twelve people a night, where do the rest of them go? There are bloody buildings that are empty. They could set it up. Pay a nightwatchman. No drugs, no alcohol. They could even charge people $2 a night. You've got to have money for accommodation [now]. Even The Sally's [The Salvation Army] used to give you a bed, but now its money up-front. They're bloody hypocrites as far as I'm concerned. Prevention for the younger ones is an important step, too.

A drop-in centre is trying to get me emergency housing now out where [a mate of mine] George is. With me medical thing I'm on priority. Last year I went fruit-picking in Victoria. In February, I woke up with a pain across me gut. I thought it was food poisoning. They took me to the hospital, gave me a shot in the arse and two tablets and sent me home. That night it got worse so I went back and they put me in. I found out I had kidney stones. He [the surgeon] said, 'We have to open you up.' They moved me kidney and bladder around and since then I can't hold me water.

I stayed at me sister's place in Victoria for a while. But, I had an argument with her husband so I packed up and came back here. But I was pissing blood. So I went to the hospital and they gave me the choice. [I chose] to kill the kidney. So we did that last year. My bladder has been acting up. It's been stretched [about] from all the surgery. So I've got another operation coming up.

Now I've got to watch what I eat. If I lose this [last] kidney I'm fucked. When they took my kidney out my name went down on a list. The surgeon said it'd be fifteen or twenty years [until a donor organ was available], but if you had $40,000 your name would go to the top; money talks. All my medical treatment is on Medicare; if it wasn't I couldn't afford it. I'm on the disability pension now.

Ray Sippel

I get $432 [a fortnight]. I live on pain-killers and blood pressure pills and antibiotics. I'm a walking bloody pharmacy!

I've been off the streets for about two weeks now. [My mate] George has been letting me stay at his place. He'd been living on the streets for about ten years himself [before being housed]. The place I'm supposed to be getting is in the same block as him, so we'll be neighbours. If I get that place I'll be laughing. It's a bed-sit, and if I get it I'll be there the rest of me life.

Ricky Cain
age 30

My father was a farmer in western Victoria until he got sick and we had to sell the property. He went one way and I went to Mum's. Then I got abused by me stepfather. I haven't spoken to them for years. I got kicked out of home when I was thirteen and I've been on the streets since then.

[When I left home] I was on the streets of Melbourne for about four years. I first stayed in squats with other people. I was with the wrong people and [got into] heroin when I was thirteen and a half. I was in gaol by fourteen. I was doing break-and-enters, getting money for drugs. [Well] it started with doing break-and-enters, then we started sticking people up with knives to get money. There was also a charge of assault with a deadly weapon. I was fourteen when we done [all] that. [The] judge didn't like it so it was straight to gaol.

Ricky Cain

I went to the Youth Training Centre [YTC] until I was seventeen. When I turned seventeen they put me in an adult gaol at Pentridge, in Melbourne. YTC was like a holiday camp [compared with Pentridge]. I shit myself the first time I went to Pentridge. I was in for five years [including time in YTC]; that was pretty bad. The first day I was pretty nervous, but I was alright, nothing happened. They put me in 'A' division, which is full of rapists and murderers. You just speak when you get spoken to, that's how I did it. Once you go to gaol you can handle that life, so you can [easily] go in again.

When I was twenty I got out. I was only out for a month and then I was back in again. Every year until 1999 I went to gaol. Sometimes it was for two weeks or [sometimes] six months or two years. I've been out [of gaol] for four years and haven't been back in since. I was still doing heroin now and then, but it wasn't like I was doing it every day, like [spending] $200 or $400 a day or anything like that. Each time [in between gaol stints] I was living on the street, in squats and whatever.

You wouldn't believe the amount of people on the streets. What kept me going [during that time] was drugs, just getting money for drugs, just a cycle. [Being homeless,] the public look down on you when you're walking along the street. They see me tattoos. Everybody takes you for what you look like, not who you are. The cops hassle me, too. They'll walk up to you [and say], 'What are yeh sitting here for?' They still stop and search me.

In 1999 me brother overdosed on heroin. That's when I thought, I've had enough of this. My brother was living with me mother and I wasn't having anything to do with them. Me sister died about ten years before [my brother] in an accident. I've got a stepbrother and two stepsisters. Now and then I'll be in contact with them.

[My brother] was into drugs before me. I went down to see him, what they called a 'viewing'. You see the body and that. I just woke up to meself, I think. I stopped hanging around with bad people and fixed meself. I went through rehab in Melbourne and that was pretty good. I've been [living] off and on in Sydney and Melbourne for years. I've been in Sydney for two years now. At the moment I'm living in a boarding house that costs $140 a week. That's not cheap. It's not the best place in Kings Cross. I'm trying to get me own [place].

Before [the boarding house] it's been squats, the street or gaol [since age thirteen]. There weren't many squats around [so] if you found one there'd probably be about twenty or thirty people in there. Most of the people in them would be in the same situation as me, from a similar background [and childhood]. [The conditions] were pretty bad in squats. [You'd find] hundreds of sticks [syringes] lying around on the ground. You'd get to a place and give it a clean. The last one I was in still had power, running water and TV. I picked up two hundred and fifty sticks [syringes] in that one. Squats are only open for a few months then they normally get locked down and you [have to] find another one.

Otherwise, there'd be an alleyway, you'd just lie down and sleep. I didn't get much sleep, though. I was worried about what was going to happen. I've had stuff robbed, nothing [else] happened [though]. You sleep with one eye open. If you're in a group [in that situation] you're better off. When you're on heroin you don't give a shit about anyone else but yourself.

Ricky Cain

It's not easy getting into a rehab program. You've gotta keep ringing them and ringing them. It took me three months to get into one, a government one. If a week goes past where you don't ring, then you get sent back [on the list]. I'd ring every second day and wait for a bed to come up. I've been having it [heroin] now and again [since the rehab]. [When I do] I go to an injection room [Sydney Medically Supervised Injecting Centre (MSIC), in Kings Cross]. They save a lot of lives. I mean, I've been in there and three or four people have OD'd. If they'd been on the streets in a back alley having it they would've been dead. [In injection rooms] they also get to use clean sticks and not dirty ones.

I'm trying to stay away from using, [but] you'd be walking down the street and all your mates are on it. You want a shot and, bang, you're on it. Eight months ago I OD'd on heroin. It was just too strong. I never OD'd before. It was scary. I just dropped [to the ground] in the park. The paramedics gave me three [adrenaline] shots to bring me back. I was never sick until I stopped taking [heroin] and then I started getting sick.

I have a child, a daughter. I was living with [the mother] for about three and a half years and then I split up with her. I met her when I was using [heroin]. She fell pregnant when we were both using. That made her stop and [helped] me stop. It makes a big difference having [my daughter]; it's something to look forward to. They live in [southern NSW]. I still see them. I want to eventually try and move down there, try and get a [Housing] Commission house. I applied for it two months ago [but] there is a two-year waiting list.

Henry Thompson
age 29

I've had a pretty much turbulent past. When I was about three months old I was given up [by my mother]. DOCS [Department of Community Services] took me and put me into Barnardos [Children's Charity]. Then I stayed with a foster family in Gosford until I was six but their circumstances changed. I went back to my mother for a short while when I was about five, but DOCS ended up coming and getting me [after] I was locked in cupboards and stuff like that.

I went [back] to Barnardos, where I stayed until I was fourteen. I was [eventually] fostered by an English family [called] the Pellings. I stayed with them until I was eighteen or nineteen. They had to move back to England: my foster mother's dad was getting really ill and they wanted to go to him. I said I wanted to stay in Australia and their kids stayed here, too.

Henry Thompson

When they left I went searching for my mum. I found she was living in Victoria. Straight from the start we just didn't get on. I went [to see her] after travelling on a bus for twelve hours, and the first thing she said to me was, 'I don't mind you staying here as long as your dole cheque comes to me.' I was shocked. I just said no and went to stay in a nearby St Vinnies [St Vincent de Paul]. I stayed there for a couple of weeks and just thought it was a waste of my time. So I came back to Sydney.

Two or three years ago I had a change of heart and I went down [to see her]. It was going okay, but then she suddenly moved. I found out that she'd moved because I knew where she lived. I'd been on the streets for about a year so I was hardened and it bounced off me. I thought, if that's the way she wants to live, well …

[My] brothers and sisters all seem to get on well with my mum. I ended up living with my sister for three months but decided to come back to Sydney. That's when I pretty much started staying on the streets full-time. I needed to fend for myself. If anyone asks I say I do have family, but I don't. We don't have contact. I do [have] feelings [towards my mother] but they're mainly feelings of anger and hurt because I just can't believe how a woman can have a child and not love it. There's always other options, like abortion.

After the Pellings left I stayed with some friends but they were starting families and I didn't want to get in the way of that. I ended up in a homeless hostel in Sydney. Then the bad thing really hit—gambling. When I started gambling the bottom of the box just dropped out [for me]. I put more and more money into gambling. By that stage I was sleeping wherever I could. I'd get to my [social welfare] payday and it'd be gone [on gambling].

Henry Thompson

Once, I was walking down George Street and all of a sudden I stopped and almost heard in my mind [the words], 'Go across the road.' I crossed and on the other side was a pay packet on the ground. It had no name on it but had $900 inside. It's like I have an alarm in my head that senses money. Last week, I was up in Martin Place and the sensor went off—whenever it does I automatically look around—I looked across and saw something in the gutter, a $100 note. When I was gambling really hard, if I found money that was it, I'd be straight into a pokies place until it was all gone.

Deep down, I knew gambling was something I didn't want to do. They have a lot of pull, the pokies, with their bright lights and sounds. They draw you in. I still occasionally drop $30 or $40 in them, but that's just a 'cure'. If someone is sick they take medication. So that's what I call my medication. I just drop in a little bit of money and that's enough. Then I just walk out the door still full of money, still healthy.

Before, I'd get up at five in the morning on a [social welfare] payday. I believe I've got an alarm in my head and every payday the alarm goes off. By eleven o'clock in the morning [my pay] would be gone. Then I'd be sitting on a bench thinking what the hell have I done? Gambling pulls you. You are thinking, should I get a feed or should I try [again]? And because you've been on a pokie machine for four hours [your head tells] you to try again so you can get your money back. But it just doesn't work.

Now I've got a couple of bad health issues and I've got to keep money aside in case [something happens]. I'm going in for surgery soon to have an abscess removed from my back. It means I'll be recovering in hospital for three months and after the operation I'll be unable to move.

To be honest, it was absolutely scary when I first started sleeping rough. I see some people on their first day [of being homeless] and they look horrified, they don't know what to make of anybody. It was the same for me. I didn't know if people were going to come and bash me. That happened to me once. I was sleeping on Observatory Hill. There was me and a Malaysian mate and we'd been sleeping there for two weeks. One night I heard the drinking fountain near us and I looked to see who it was. That was the start of the trouble.

There were three big Pacific Islanders and they came up and said, 'What are you staring at? We were having a drink and you were star- ing at us.' I told them I just heard a sound, looked up and looked back. But as soon as they came out with that question I knew some- thing was going to happen. I told them we had no money, that we were homeless. They didn't want to listen. I turned to me mate [as they neared] and told him, 'When I say run, run. I'm not joking.'

Next thing, one of them got me [and] kicked me in the head and punched me. I've got a rock for a head so I don't know if it was the adrenaline, but I didn't feel any of it. I just ran. I told my mate to run and he ran. I ran down to the nearest cop shop and told them what happened.

I went back [to Observatory Hill] and my mate was up there asleep. I said, 'Tim, you alright?' He pulled his head out and he had this lump on his head the size of a golf ball. He didn't know where he was. I called an ambulance for him. After those guys attacked us, they attacked a Chinese couple that were on the other side of the hill, just a couple gone for a romantic walk! They bashed the guy and nearly beat the girl to death. It just amazes me how people can do that. All they did it for was money.

A lot of things have happened that have made me harder. I was woken up one morning with a knife at my throat. Not to pick on certain [types of] people, but he was a junkie. I woke up and felt the metal against my throat. I could feel the shape of the knife. My hands were underneath the covers so I raised one arm out. When junkies are hanging out for their gear [heroin] they can be twitchy, and he was very twitchy. As he was twitching I grabbed his hand and pulled the knife out of it. I dare say I gave him the beating of his life. But I was just defending myself. Nobody is going to like waking up to a knife at their throat. When [people] do things like that, I can't understand. I mean, get it into your head; the main reason I'm on the street is because I don't have money! If I did have money I'd prefer to leave it in the bank than have it on me.

I'm pretty sure I stayed [my] first night on the street at Town Hall Station. There's a little park on the side of Town Hall Square. Every move I heard that night I woke up. It's a terrifying feeling for someone that has just come out on the street. There were other people [sleeping in the park], too. After a couple of nights, one bloke saw me shivering. He had two or three blankets so he gave me one. He just said, 'You need this, take it.' I started talking to him, had a cigarette and when the older ones saw that they came over [and joined us]. We formed a close-knit little community in there. They all agreed if any us got touched by anyone [such as muggers] the others would jump on the attacker.

Henry Thompson

It's just amazing how people in the same situation can bond. [When] I left that group there were no hard feelings or anything. They all sort of said, 'Well, you've got to go and do your own thing.' If I run into them we still say g'day [although] some of them are gone now.

I finally found an area under a bridge in Darling Harbour and started sleeping there. Over time I started getting new friends and they'd come down there, too. I'm the sort of person where I don't like getting cold, so I found a little mattress, it may have been a cot mattress. I had a sheet to go over that and the blankets. I've never had to look for a blanket [because] I've got blankets stashed all around the city in case it rains or if someone steals them. I was there [under the bridge] for about six months. Sometimes you get rumbled [caught] so I have to keep moving every couple of weeks.

There has been a few stages where I've got myself rooms. The first time I got a room I was paying $155 a week, which would leave me with $80 [for the rest of the fortnight]. The thing that capped it off [there] was I woke up with the [building] caretaker standing in my room at five in the morning. He just left and I went back to sleep. [Later] I went downstairs and said to him, 'What the hell were you doing in my room this morning?' He [wouldn't really] answer me. That was totally illegal, he shouldn't have come in without knocking or getting my permission. After that I moved out. Another time I rented a room out at Petersham [for] $130 a week for three months. But the gambling stuffed me on that one.

I call the spot I'm in now 'the jungle'. It is down behind Darling Harbour. I just moved there two weeks ago. That's the best I've had yet. It's peaceful. I don't bother anybody and I can do whatever I want. I've got the fence and nobody is going to walk down the monorail tracks. Sometimes workmen go past and you hear this whipper snipper go off five metres from your head! They don't mind [me being there]; they just say, 'Stay there, you're cool.' They know I'm not impeding their job.

I even had a workman come up one morning. I was still sleeping because I was a bit crook. He came up to me and said, 'Here, do you want this?' He handed me a meat pie and a can of drink. That is a real genuine person, someone who will do that without even questioning you.

I got drunk once and ended up falling asleep in the park down in Darling Harbour. The first thing this security guard said to me was, 'What the fuck are you doing sleepin' here?' I was still a bit tipsy and I said, 'Mate, I got drunk and I wandered down here with my friends and fell asleep in the park.' It was totally by accident because, you know, I already had my spot [where I slept, elsewhere].

One time, I was sleeping at Darling Harbour and I was seen by the security guards and they were real rough. I was carrying my stuff and my mattress in front of me and a security guard is behind me pushing me, [telling me] 'Go faster! Go faster!' I got to the end [of the pavement] and he pushed me and I accidentally trod on the end of my blanket and fell over. I landed on the mattress, but I also landed on the road. If a car had come along I would have been cleaned up! So I got up and went across the road. I was in a huff and ripped my jumper off and said, 'You've got an attitude problem, mate. If you want to have a go, come over here!' I'd had enough.

Henry Thompson

He was trying to get me to fight back when I was in his area [of jurisdiction]. As soon as I was across the road they walked off. He knew that if I had nothing in my hands I was going to stand up to him. He probably would've smashed me, but that's not the point. I've spoken to security guards that are real sweet, really good to talk to, but these blokes? I don't know, I think the name of the company [must be] Arrogance Incorporated.

Countless times security guards tell me that I shouldn't be here. Why shouldn't I be here? I always like to [set my place up] out of the way. I don't like it when people can see me. I told [a guard] once, 'Take a look around, there's no-one who can see me. I'm just sleeping here.'

That's why I don't stay outside the NSW Library, there's too many people walking past and I don't like people being able to see me. I don't mind if they're in the distance, as long as it's difficult for them to get to me. I'll make sure there's a six-foot-high fence in the way but I'll know how to get through it easily. I'll take a couple of bolts off [the fence] and open it like a door, then close and bolt it [behind me]. That's my security.

I've had plenty of times when I've come back to my place and everything I've got is gone. So I have to go to a stash, get some blankets and start again. The other week I got back and there was a bloke going through my stuff. I had to chase him [shouting], 'If I get my hands on you, you'll be sorry!' It was just for show so he wouldn't think about coming back, which he hasn't.

Some people don't want to open their eyes to the homeless. There are so many places where people like me can sleep, undetected.

Henry Thompson

The [spot at] the NSW Library is getting worse and they're starting to close it all off so they can't sleep there. The spot I had down in Town Hall was between two pillars. They've put doors there now to stop people [sleeping there]. It wasn't because of homeless people; you'd walk past and see needles lying around.

I stayed for two months outside the Domain Car Park. You don't see as many homeless people there now. I don't think the authorities liked it. We were there one night and this flash Holden Statesman [car] pulls up. This plump lady gets out and walks all the way down [the car park] seeing every homeless person. There would have been over ten of us there. I thought she was going around shaking people's hands, which would be nice. You know like, at least somebody's thinking of you. She comes up to me and hands me $50 and says, 'Go get yourself a feed.' She had given everyone at the Domain a $50 note each. Afterwards we were still wondering whether it was real [so] we went off to the shop and no worries, it was real alright!

Some people just walk past. Some people give you a look. I get a lot of the women grabbing their bags [when they see me]. One day, I had enough [of that]. I was walking through Pitt Street Mall and every woman I walked past grabbed her bag. One woman grabbed it so obviously that I turned around to her and said, 'Excuse me ma'am, I would never, ever snatch someone's handbag.' She just [looked at me apologetically and said], 'Oh sorry, I must have mistook you for the wrong type of person.' I told her everybody does. There's no way I'm going to attack a woman to get some money. Nor would I bash a guy for money.

Henry Thompson

One night, this bloke near Pitt Street bolted past me and I see this lady running. So I ran after him and tackled him and got the woman's bag back. A couple of big Maori fellas came over and held him down until the coppers came along. She offered me $20 to get a feed. I didn't take it because at the time I had a little bit of money. I'd help people in a second [if they needed it].

Another time near Market City [in the CBD] there was a bloke and he had a girl inside a doorway. He was holding her right up against the wall and full-out yelling at her like a man would [to another man]. I tapped him on the shoulder and he turned on me and said, 'What the fuck do you want?' I said, 'You're talking to a man now, watch your mouth!' I took a few steps back as if to take him on and he just walked off. I asked the woman if she was alright. She told me that he'd wanted her to go somewhere she didn't want to go. She was shaking, so I said, 'Do you want me to get you a taxi?' I got her a taxi and she's gone off and I just wandered on my way. If any woman is in trouble I will always go to their aid because it's not fair for a man to pick on a woman.

When I was a heavy gambler losing [money] all the time, I [gave up] and just thought I'd stay there [in the heavy gambling situation I was in]. I was gambling every cent I had for eighteen months. What really inspired me to give up gambling was when two years ago I got my fortnightly dole payment of $480 and the [Centrelink] $500 loan. I went into a pub near Central [Station] in the morning and left at eleven that night with nothing.

When you [finally] stop doing things like that you can see the improvement. So I [got] a car, a Cortina. I had my licence. I had a place to stay. It was only a caravan, but who cares? To me it's a house. It's got a roof. I loved it. I had a girlfriend at the time. We put our money together and bought the car. It was $900 but I got it for $750. I'm a perfectionist with cars. As soon as I got it I had to give it a good scrub everywhere. The funniest thing was I cleaned the back and got $3 or $4 from behind the back seat. Then doing the carpeting I saw this rip and lifted it up [to find] $350 in $50 notes! So we used that to go on a holiday. We bought a tent and an esky and drove out into the middle of nowhere. It was good to have seen that change, because now I can look at the future and say, 'This is what I did last time.'

I think my relationships die because I've been stung too many times. It gets on your feelings when [that happens]. [Eventually] you see the next woman and you think, is she going to sting me again? That is a bad way to think because you can break up with somebody that is genuinely good for you, but you've just got it in your head that she's going to sting you. I think my childhood [affected that]. I'm [also] very shy, but I'm starting to come 'round.

I want to get rid of the gambling and some of these medical problems and start doing what I should be doing. More or less, restart or kick-start my life. I'm twenty-nine and I should be settled down with a family [by now]. I want to get a stable place to live and hopefully a relationship with my father.

In a couple of years if I can be free of gambling I'm hoping to move to Brisbane because I think that's where my father is. I'm in the prime of my life where next year I'm turning thirty and it'll be good to know who my father is. I know him by name, but that's all I know. It'd be good to meet him face-to-face. I've not seen any photos. I wouldn't know what he looks like. I've tried to recollect that time but it's too far back. When I try to remember I get images of my mother locking me up in things so I think, no more. I'm not going to think of it.

I've also got to set myself for [the possibility of] him not wanting to meet me, although I'll be wanting an excuse why. After twenty-nine years without having met him an explanation is needed. It's reasonable [to expect one]. I'll be upset if he says that it was his doing; that he just left. But I won't be so angry if I found out it was my mum that pushed him out. In my head that's the only logical [reason] I [can see]. It would be really good to meet him, that's all I can say.

Dave Wilson
age 42

I was adopted at four months [of age] by a working-class couple in Adelaide. I was their second adopted son; my brother was also adopted by them. When I was about four we moved to Darwin for a couple of years. My father worked for the government and he got transferred to Canberra, where I did the majority of my growing up. I stayed there until I was seventeen and finished school. From there I went to Sydney, and then Byron Bay for about year, and returned to Sydney for twenty years. I was working for most of it.

The first time I went up to Lismore (near Byron Bay) I was nineteen and I met this girl. There was very little work up there [so] we moved back down to Sydney. Sydney was the big magnet, mainly because of work and money. We ended up getting married pretty young. I was twenty-three and she was a year older. We had a child straight away, a son. For a while when she was pregnant, and for six or twelve months after she had the baby, I was working two jobs keeping the money coming in. Things just rolled along for a while. Over a period of time we just grew apart.

The fights [between us] became more heated and more frequent. We didn't want our son growing up in that bullshit environment because we'd both grown up with parents fighting, too. We loved our son too much to want him to grow up in that environment so we split [up]. It was a major turning point in my life. She moved out [with our son] and I hung onto the place for a while, but it was too big [for one person]. I had too much stuff. I needed a truck to move it. I realised how ridiculous it was, one person having that much stuff. I gradually started travelling lighter, to the point where I lived out of a bag.

That was really the beginning. It was the major fork in my life that led to homelessness over a period of time. From the marriage breaking up, becoming homeless probably took about ten years. After the break-up I eventually started dabbling in drugs, heavy drugs like coke [cocaine] and heroin. Ultimately, my drug of choice was heroin.

As I started travelling lighter and dabbling in a bit of crime I became really mobile. It wasn't unusual for me. I think people working in the drug rehab field call it 'doing the geographical'—to move around from city to city. If you live in a city for a long period of time and get into a drug rut you think, if I go to Melbourne I'll be okay because I won't know any dealers there and I won't know the drug crowd and everything will be sweet. But what happens is that you find those [kinds of] people without consciously meaning to. I've gone to hick towns in the middle of nowhere and within hours of getting off the bus I know who the heroin addicts are just by walking down the street and checking people out, especially if you want to score. It's like a radar. I've heard that people who use [heroin] give off this weird sort of energy. You just learn to pick people by experience.

I first started getting into coke, eckies [ecstasy pills] and speed [amphetamine], stuff like that. You start taking drugs to counter-act the drugs [that you've already taken]. It was like cutting an umbilical cord to my past. I was never really good at dealing with my feelings and getting over the marriage break-up. I just couldn't deal with it. I didn't really have time to. In the modern world you've got to go to work, got to be here, be there. You don't have time to breathe. You've just got to bury it. Heroin is the perfect drug to bury feelings. When you stop using, those feelings bubble to the surface again and you've got to deal with it somewhere along the track. You can keep burying those feelings for twenty years; some people never deal with it.

[As time went on] I got sacked from jobs. I worked in travel agencies. Part of my job was picking up people's tickets and pass-ports and delivering it to them. I fucked up that a few times. I'd be waiting to meet a dealer somewhere and they would make me wait for an hour and I'd be late with the tickets [for work]. Eventually I got a call into the office and that was that.

I never ripped off any people I worked for, though. Over a period of time you just learn to hustle. I was always good at hustling, even if it was legal shit. I mean, a lot of legal stuff is hustling, too. I got pretty good at shoplifting. In a way it's like a victimless crime. I'd only steal from big department stores and they factor shoplifting into their prices. Even if people stopped shoplifting tomorrow they wouldn't reduce the prices.

It didn't cut up my conscience too much. Occasionally I did a bit of fraud. It was stuff like that, but there was never any violent shit. Occasionally I'd supplement it with a bit of dealing. With dealing I only ever would sell to four or five people, just enough to keep my habit going. I never introduced anybody to it. I never pushed it on anyone. The people I sold to were long-term users, I gave them good deals and I didn't rip them off.

I squatted for a couple of years. I love the politics of squatting, too. It comes back to the whole concept of ownership. I understand the machinations of the whole capitalist system. I could probably sit just as happily on the other side of the fence if I'd been born into money. There is a justification for rent. But there's a justification for not paying it, too. That's what squatters do. A lot of the time they're only making use of places that are just sitting there. So I got into that for a fair while.

That's why I was based in Melbourne for five years. The squatting scene was a lot better there. That led to homelessness, when the squatting [element] was out of the equation. It was a shock [being without a place]. There'd been odd nights when I was about fifteen when I just had to fuck off on me own because I was so afraid of me old man. He would get physical and that's why I split [originally] and I had to sleep out.

I don't think there'd be many guys who've been homeless for longer than five minutes, especially young guys, who haven't had some sort of sleazy homosexual experience. You get some weirdo that comes up and goes, 'You wanna come back to my place?' or even just try to rub you up then and there. Or just guys coming home drunk from the pub going, 'Let's kick the shit out of this bloke!' There was an old [homeless] guy up the cross [that] these guys soaked in metho [methylated spirits] and burned alive. It's like [the novel], *A Clockwork Orange*.

Even in squats sometimes people try to heavy in on the squat. They [might] want to take over or rip you off or they just want to fuck you up. You've got to be pretty conscious of security in squats, even [of] your own personal stuff, because you get all types of people. Generally the camaraderie among squatters is pretty good. I mean, ultimately, you can get ripped off by anybody. A lawyer with all the money in the world can still end up with a bad coke habit and rip off a stereo. That sort of stuff happens [whether it's] in Double Bay or Mt Druitt.

Sleeping on the street [and not in squats] was something I always tried to avoid, even to the point where me and this guy slept in the engine room of a lift in an old building for about four months. That'd be the most bizarre place I've ever slept in. [The lift] was still active [so] it was deafening. The [other] guy, who lived there first, had rigged two bits of wire to hold up a door. He had it hanging there so he could sleep above all the machinery [like a bunk]. I literally had to sleep between the wall, next to the door, and the machinery [of the motor]. I had to sleep on my side and be careful not to roll over too far and have my arm end up in the machine!

Sometime after midnight we'd turn the machine off so people would have to walk up the stairs. That was probably our undoing. Even though we got a good run there, enough people complained,

Dave Wilson

'How come the fuckin' lift isn't working late at night?' So [the building management] went up and checked and went, 'Fuck! People are living there!'

For a few weeks after that we had to resort to staying in the [drunk] tanks [Proclaimed Places[4]]. It was like that Pogues song, 'Christmas in New York', where they talk about waking up in the drunk tank. You'd just rock up there and go, 'Uh, I'm really pissed!' In some cases they let you in even if they know you're stoned. The drunk tanks are something else; it reminded me of some sort of Hieronymus Bosch vision of hell. Occasionally you just get psychos there, because a lot of the [mental] asylums are just booting people out and they just hit the street and end up in places like that.

Shit, I hated the drunk tanks. I mean I handled it—that was about the best thing you could do. It was interesting from a sort of existential perspective, but fuck that wears off pretty quick! I felt the same way when I was nineteen about gaol, because you hear all these horror stories [about gaol]. You think, fuck, is it really that bad? [With] your male ego there is always a part of you that thinks, I'd like to see if I could survive that. I did probably two years of gaol [myself] all up, in six-month stints from drug [charges] over a period of years from 1996 to 2000. It was interesting. I ended up going to most of the big gaols in NSW, like Goulburn, Long Bay, Parramatta and Grafton.

The funny thing, well, it didn't turn out that funny, was when they initially locked me up. In those first twelve hours or so [of being] locked up I got more and more anxious, to the point where I was in a state of panic. The first opportunity I got I was over the fence, or over three fences! About three weeks later they got me.

Then, once I'd been charged with escape I automatically got what's called a 'needs classification', which means I'm an escapee. Even if I only got six months [gaol time] I had to do it all in maximum [security]. But in a way I didn't mind, because I thought, well at least the gaol I do is going to be real gaol. It's not going to be some farm where you've got these guys that are there for hitting their wife. You've got the real fuckin' hardcore guys and you've got to find out real quick what the rules are and don't break 'em or they'll break you. Most of these guys aren't insane. If you're criminally insane you're off to somewhere else. It's funny—there are probably more rules in gaol than there are outside. It's not anarchy [in gaol]; it's very ordered in a lot of ways.

One of the big myths about gaol is about homosexual rape; that's bullshit. It's something that cops threaten young kids with, saying, 'You don't wanna break the law or you'll end up in gaol and you know what'll happen to you.' The only sex that I was aware of in gaol was totally consensual. There are a lot of fairies in gaol and that's fine. The only way I could see someone being raped in gaol would be as a type of punishment, a way of humiliating them for something that they'd done, which they may or may not deserve. But most people who have studied the phenomenon of rape say it is about power, it's not about sex.

[Since the last time I got out of gaol] there's not been a lot of contact with my family, just the odd phone call. I haven't got much family left and they're spread all over the place. When you're using [heroin] and leading the sort of lifestyle I've lived for the last ten years you tend to lose contact with people. You don't want to impose your chaos on people who are leading the straight and narrow [life]. Sometimes you want to [contact them]. It's just something you're constantly weighing up. You think, is it worth it, the effect of it all? With my son there has been the odd phone call and the odd letter. [It's okay] with my ex-wife. [Having that contact] makes a bit of a difference.

Counting squatting, [I've] been on the streets about fifteen years. [Actually] *on* the streets it's probably ten [years]. I might sleep the odd night in a park or on the beach sometimes in summer. But generally I try to find a squat or a shelter. There are even a few caves not far from the city. There's one in Potts Point.

I've been on methadone [treatment] for a few years, although I still have the occasional shot [of heroin], but very rarely, and now I'm starting to come off the methadone as well. I put off going on [methadone] for fifteen years and I was always against it. For me it was just replacing one drug with another drug. It was like government-legalised heroin. Liquid handcuffs. A way of the government knowing where you were and what you were doing.

Everything about it [heroin] repulsed me, but I just reached a point where I had a big habit and I wanted to stop doing crime because I didn't want to go back to gaol. I thought I'd just go on this stuff [methadone] for a week or two, long enough to get the heroin out of me but not long enough to get addicted to the methadone. What happened was I got arrested and I got six months for stuff I'd already done before going on the methadone. It happens, it catches up [with you] at some point. Anyway, I got six months and because I was in maximum [security] I knew there was going to be some days where I [would be] locked up for twenty-three hours. Being on the methadone made it easier, and before I knew it I'd been on methadone [for] six months. It made doing the gaol [time] easier because it knocks you out. So before I knew it, three or four years had gone [by], but you know, there's light at the end of the tunnel.

Initially [after the last time in gaol] I went to [a place] like a tank. It's quite a big complex and they've got a couple of rooms for guys who are more together than the guys who stay in the tank and they charge you rent. You get a bit more freedom; you can come and go when you want. It's a step up. They help you get your own place. I'll be moving in there [soon].

[To help people on the streets] they've got to do it in gradual stages. They've got to realise that people who've been on the streets for any length of time are damaged in some way. They can't move from stage to stage and situation to situation with the freedom that other people can. It's just like learning to crawl and walk again. Some people are going to be awfully slow to start with and then they'll just power [on].

For me [the will to change] was a combination of things I weighed up over time. But also, a big inspiration over the last twelve months was a guy, a mate, we were like best buddies. There was three of us, actually. This guy kept pushing and pushing for somewhere to live. The [other] two of us weren't pushing that much at the time and he finally cracked it and got his own flat. Even though he had nothing [in his flat] for the first month or two—he was looking at four walls because he'd been living on the street for five years or so—everything gradually started falling into place once he got that flat.

Dave Wilson

He stopped using [heroin]. He reduced [his] methadone to the point where he's been off it totally for the last month. He's started getting a bit of work. Initially it was just volunteer work but it became paid work. He reunited with his family. He's like my immediate role model, because a year ago he was in exactly the same position I am in now. He's a great mate of mine and I love him and respect him. I found that inspiring, because a couple of months before he got the place I was really worried about him. He was so far down in a rut but he snapped out of it.

The government and people in government that can do something about housing have got to realise how important it is. It is really important. Sometimes they [the government] might lose the feeling as to why it is important, but believe me it is. The reason is because the best asset of a country is its people, not what you can grow in the ground or what you pull out of it, but the people. Every great idea, movement, book, picture, film, you name it, has come from the people. A person that has been looked after and cared for, loved, nurtured, educated and been allowed to grow in a society can ultimately make untold money. [The government people might wonder] when are we going to get a return on spending money on these people? Well, you will get it if you follow it up. Just don't throw money at it and think it will cure everything. You've got to get people to work in the field that really give a shit, because there are people working in the field that don't. People who are in a position who need help can spot them almost instinctively.

Mike Reeves
age 50

I grew up in eastern Sydney with my five brothers and sisters. My years of growing up were pretty good; I came from a very strict Catholic upbringing. I still had a normal childhood and got up to mischief like any kid does. A lot of my early childhood was filled with illness. I was in and out of hospital a few times. I had tuberculosis when I was very young and then I suffered from a kidney ailment when I was nine years old, which I'd had since birth. I had to have major surgery for it [where] they replaced the tubes from my kidneys. It was a big hassle being nine and in hospital for months on end.

When I left school my very first job was delivering telegrams with what was called then the PMG [Postmaster-General's Department], which is Australia Post today, riding around on a bicycle in my local area delivering telegrams. I wasn't quite sixteen when I started that job and I was getting something like $190 a fortnight. I was only paying about $20 a fortnight of board to my mum. I was in that for about five years and went on to be a postman after that.

[Eventually] I moved on and tried to do something more with my life. I went to work at a Japanese trading company in Sydney in 1973, when I was twenty. They were trading all sorts of things and I was buying wool on speculation. But I only worked there for nine months because Australia had a big downturn in the wool [industry]. I was retrenched but I walked into the shipping business, not having any experience at all. I stayed for ten years doing banking and documentation until they closed up their Sydney operation.

After that, I decided to head overseas at the beginning of the 1980s. It was originally planned as a working holiday and I ended up to being in London for six years. I was working in the travel industry and I was seeing the world, travelling around on double-decker buses through Europe and meeting heaps of fun people. It was a party all of the time—that [time] was a ball!

I came back [because] there were problems within the family; my mum was dying. For a little while I was her sole carer and then she went into a nursing home. I went into the shipping industry again for a different company. It was hard looking after Mum [as] she was suffering from Alzheimer's disease. For five years, between work, I looked after her. It was a very hard slog. Living with somebody that has Alzheimer's, especially your mother, who you naturally love very much, is a very, very traumatic thing to go through. Unless you've been there and done it, no-one can talk about it.

I had bits of help from my family. My eldest sister liked to think she was running the show and would tell me how to do things.

She's been like that all my life! I'm still the little boy of the family to her, at fifty!

After all that, I resigned from the shipping job and went into the printing industry, labouring and die-cutting, making labels for soft drink bottles and things like that. I consider myself lucky that I have done all those [different] jobs. I've had a wide range of experience in my life; I haven't been [tied] down to the one area of work all the time. Having those jobs, and especially working in travel, made it very easy for me to be able to communicate with people.

The first really major relationship I had with a woman was when my mum had Alzheimer's. After about two years we broke up and I started to go through a lot of trauma with depression and that. [My problems] certainly stemmed from that period of caring for my mother. The depression started with periods of being really, really low and not wanting to do anything. I was taking time off work all the time, then going to the pub and getting drunk. That's when alcohol became a big issue for me. I think I began to use it like a crutch.

The depression progressed gradually and then I started working for State Transit, where I worked for nearly ten years. Working for them was not the easiest job, that's for sure! I worked at the same bus depot with lots of people who I got along with, but managers were always a problem for me. I was a shit-stirrer and I was a union man. There were one or two managers who I thought were absolute bastards, I won't mention names, but I had a couple of other managers who were really good.

But [the managers] always used to be on my tail because I was a union man. I would put my foot down and complain about anything. I'd always been in union work ever since I first started in shipping. The first shipping company I went into I was nominated as the office union rep [representative]. All my working life I'd been interested in fighting for workers' rights. I always saw it as 'them versus us', and for me, I was one of the little people. I was always working class. That was the way I was brought up. I found it was always a fight to get the little man's rights. The gap between the 'haves' and the 'have-nots' is getting wider every year now. All you've got to do is see the people on the streets. I've seen more of that in the last ten years than I have in the rest of my life.

The job I had at State Transit was fuelling buses. It was an interesting job in some ways and boring in others. When the buses came in you had to fuel them and operate the vacuum, which took all the rubbish out. Then, you had to put the buses through the wash and park them. That would start at five o'clock in the afternoon and go through until one o'clock in the morning.

During that time the alcohol was growing worse. I never really missed any time with work in that job as far as alcohol was concerned, but as soon as I'd knock off work I'd go home with some tinnies. I was also in a relationship with a lady and we were living together. Halfway through the relationship we were starting to fight a lot because she didn't like the hours I was working and things would just grow until we had another bust-up.

My first experience of depression really started at the end of my relationship. That's the first time I ever attempted suicide. It was the combination of having to be around a parent with Alzheimer's, work, and then the relationship break-up. It was the alcohol that started first, but I got to such a down period I didn't want to go on any more. That's when I ended up swallowing three bottles of sleeping tablets.

A friend found me and I was in very deep sleep for a few days before I came out of it. Then, for the first time, I was admitted to a psychiatric ward. I woke up in the hospital and my first thought was, shit, it didn't work! I definitely wanted to go through with it [the suicide] at the time.

When I woke up, because of the number of tablets I'd taken, I ended up very ill actually I got double pneumonia from it. So I was in the [hospital] wards for about seven weeks before I was sent down to the psych ward. I didn't have any choice [to enter the psychiatric ward] they just scheduled me. The psychiatrist came up to me in the [hospital ward]— introduced himself and said, 'You're going to come down to see us after you leave the ward'. I said, 'Ha! Over my dead body!' He said, 'It probably will be if you keep this up!' It was fright tactics, of course. The day came when I had to go down there, and I tried to bolt out of the hospital and got caught by security.

The first time I hated it because I didn't really think I needed to be there and there were times where I refused to take medication and was really drugged for the refusal to do so. Sometimes, when you're in a psychiatric ward you get to feeling, I don't need this; I'm okay to go home. Then [when you get angry] they hold you down and give you an injection. [Looking back] I don't have any bad feelings towards them; this was the result of suicide attempts and it was just the way it was.

I went into the psych ward because my family wanted me to. It started a lot of hatred between me and my family. When I first came out I thought, yeah, I probably did need that. I was going through a very bad period of my life and I did want to take my life. It helped and it didn't [help]; because even when they discharged me I was still suffering major depression, which resulted in a couple more suicide attempts and going back in again. I was admitted three times, for about a month each time. This was all in the late 1980s.

The third time, I was in there for about six weeks. They lock you in when you're getting out of hand. It was sort of like a prison, everywhere was locked doors and high fences. But there was a lot more counselling. When I was released I started to feel okay again but got back into the grog.

Every suicide attempt I used a different method. I even tried to jump off the Sydney Harbour Bridge one time. I climbed the bridge and tried to jump [off] but the coppers got me. They hauled me down the steps feet first and threw me in the back of a paddy wagon and took me to the hospital.

After I'd finished my job with State Transit, my homelessness started. I'd gotten a compensation payout and was still going through my period of depression. What money I did have, I squandered on alcohol and having a good time with women and drink. I'd been drinking for twenty years. I was living in a boarding house and didn't have a job. My period of homelessness began in the late part of the 1990s.

The first night I was homeless I was in the city sleeping on a bench. I was shit-scared and lots of things were going through my mind, from what my family would think to what I felt of myself. I met a lot of other homeless guys and we used to hang around together. We got into trouble with alcohol and violence; there were fights because of the alcohol. I've had people try to lay into me. I remember waking up one night and having some guy trying to bash me for no reason! It was in the middle of the city, at Town Hall.

For months we slept outside Town Hall Police Station. We slept there because we felt it was safe [because] the coppers were around. They didn't move us on, but the council used to. They'd come through at three or four o'clock in the morning with the cleaners going, 'Go off! Get off!' We couldn't go back afterwards because it was all wet. We just had to hang around until one of the first [homeless drop-in centres] opened, which was a place called The Station [Drop-in Centre], near Wynyard Station. You'd go [there] for breakfast, have a shower and wash your clothes. I used to spend most of the day there actually; [you could] watch TV and get free meals. It wasn't bad. I used to get to know the guys who did the cooking and they were pretty good people.

On the streets I saw violence. I saw theft, drug overdoses, a number of things. The hardest part was sleeping with one eye open. You're constantly watching out for yourself. I heard of an incident down near Matthew Talbot [Hostel] where there were quite a few bashings by some guys dressed up like something out of *The Matrix*.

It never ceases to amaze me, the attitude of people towards the homeless, where you are treated as if you are a sixth-grade person. As for the police, I personally never had any problems. They might hassle you every now and then but they never really caused me any problems because I always tried to do the right thing and say, 'Yes sir. No sir.'

With the general public, you only have to see the way they look at you. When you're homeless the way they look at you is with utter contempt. The harshest part was the long days with nothing to do but trying to survive. It was extremely depressing.

One of the things that used to embarrass me about going to The Station [Drop-in Centre] was when you'd be waiting outside the door first thing in the morning. A lot of the buses would come from the old depot where I used to work, and quite a few times, guys who I used to work with would recognise me standing there. I was just so embarrassed. I spoke to a couple [of them] and they couldn't understand or failed to understand. Their initial reaction was one of shock and disbelief, because they'd known me for ten years and knew me as a steady guy.

Contact with my family was almost non-existent. It was both of our choice, more so them than myself. It was a result of my suicide attempts and the alcohol. [The lack of contact] just made it worse, because it ended up in more depression again.

The group [of homeless men] I did make friends with really stuck together and looked out for one another. Then came a period of time where I thought, I've really got to get away from these people because the alcohol is getting really bad. I mean, we were drinking three or four casks of wine a day. We would end up sleeping in what they call PPs [Proclaimed Places[4]]. They became a place to sleep at night because there was a roof over your head, a bed, a shower and a feed you didn't have to pay for.

Matthew Talbot [Hostel] did have one [PP] but it doesn't any more. I used to mainly stay at Campbell House. There's not many shelters left open any more and [the numbers of them] are dropping. It's [from] a direct lack of government funding, especially with this right-wing government we have at the moment that refuses to acknowledge the rate of homeless, drug and alcohol problems. They pretend [the problem] is not there and sweep it under the carpet [as if] it doesn't exist.

The amount of places for women is very limited, too. There's one or two [places] around the Cross but that's about it, as far as I know. I can't say I know of any women's places in the suburbs, so the women have to come to the city.

When you're a homeless man you don't really have contact with homeless women. It's rare to see them out there. I used to know two or three who were sleeping in Hyde Park. I also knew a guy who was sleeping in the passageway tunnels at the back of St James Station. I slept in PPs because it was safe and you could wash, but you had to leave by six o'clock in the morning and then begin your day again.

When I was staying at Campbell House and heard it was going to close down I thought, it's time I really did something with my life, I've got to get back on my feet. I met this guy who used to come to Campbell House as well; a guy called Kevin. We both decided we wanted to get a place together and that's when I first came to Rough Edges [Community Centre]. They helped me and Kevin get our first place at a boarding house. It was a relief because we were starting to live normal lives again.

I got into being a volunteer at Rough Edges [Community Centre], serving behind the [food] counter. Talking to people is one of your main things; to be there and understand what people are going through and chat with them and give them coffee at the same time. My experience of homelessness has helped me relate to these people in every way. You treat people the way you want to be treated yourself. I understand what these people are about, where they're coming from.

Now, one of my sisters and I are basically getting on okay. Before coming to Rough Edges me and my sister had really dropped off all contact. It was the counsellor at Rough Edges who encouraged me to make contact again.

Homelessness did affect my confidence and pride. Your esteem gets so low and it takes so long to get that back again. Day by day you start growing back your confidence. You start piecing things back together. You get everything working for you, financially. That's why you have your caseworker, such as I did at Foster House.

Long-term homelessness in a lot of cases is [a matter of] choice. You can get help if you want it. I was at Foster House and that's run by The Salvation Army. I found the way they treat you there is incredibly good. They have rules that you have to abide by—no alcohol, no drugs, and you've got to be in by a certain time of night—but it's just putting discipline back in your life again. Homelessness can be caused by a lot of things, relationship breakdowns, depression, suicide or alcohol. All those things contribute to homelessness and to the delay of getting out of it again.

My view [on the funding of homelessness] is that the government needs a bloody big kick up the arse. They [politicians] need to get off their right-wing arses and really take a look at what's going on all over Australia. The politicians have got to be able to change people's minds on homelessness in a humane, understanding, caring way. I'd like to sit down with John Howard, and instead of him rattling off like he always does I'd like to say, 'Shut the fuck up and listen to me for a while—and don't talk until I'm finished! I've been there, done that, sunshine!' Or [say it to] Peter Costello, who I consider an idiot.

There should be conferences where homeless people can speak to the government and their local representative and tell them how it really is and for these dickheads to sit down and fucking listen. They get up on TV and talk about their own ideas [when] they have no idea.

The [previous] Lord Mayor of Sydney, [Lucy] Turnbull, used to go on about how she was going to clean up Kings Cross, get rid of the homeless people, close down the injecting centre and move the girls off the street because they were an eyesore. The woman has probably never been in Kings Cross in her bloody life! She wouldn't have the first idea what's it's like [and has] never spent time walking along Darlinghurst Road and talking to the people.

I have a bad view of [current Lord Mayor] Clover Moore. We were going to have a major development at St John [the Evangelist in Darlinghurst] and Rough Edges [Community Centre]. In the beginning, Clover Moore was right behind the development because we were going to get a big new Rough Edges. We were going to expand and help more people. But then all the yuppies around here started going on about how it would be bad for the [local] environment and she changed her mind.

Over the next few years I see myself still being at Rough Edges. A while ago, it was talked about that certain volunteers could be trained and moved into counselling, so hopefully I can do that. We haven't had any movement on that yet. We do a little bit, in a way, especially when you're working four nights a week from eight o'clock to eleven-thirty. I think I have the ability to talk to people on their own level, but I also have the ability to not take bullshit from anybody.

With my family I've moved on and gained control of my emotions. I'm at the point where if that's the [place] where they want to be, that's their undoing, not mine. I've got a life to live. I've got to move on and not stay down in the depth of depression because of it.

Having come to Rough Edges has totally changed my life. The counsellors have become my family and shown me a way to get on with my life. They've also brought God back into my life. I find now that I'm among people who love and care for me and I feel exactly the same way about them. They are my family.

Todd Parker
age 27

I grew up on the Central Coast with me mum, me brother and sister. I don't know me dad; he took off when I was six months old. Mum didn't take things too well [afterwards]; that's why she kicked me out when I was about fifteen. We weren't getting on and I wasn't doing well in school, I wasn't concentrating enough. So I left home and came to Sydney. When I first arrived it was pretty hard [because] I had to find a place to live. I spent a couple of nights on the streets, just in a park.

The first couple of nights were weird and cold. I think it was autumn. I didn't really get to sleep [but] I didn't think about going back home. I just wanted to be on me own for a while. Then [after the first couple of nights] I thought, bugger this, I'm going to find meself a refuge. I got onto some mates and they said [that I should] just go to the Marrickville Refuge. It was easy getting in [and] I stayed there for three months. I just plodded on and went from one refuge to another refuge. I also stayed on the streets and in squats.

[Over that time] I did a bit of crime: car stealing, break and enter. I got into trouble for that; ended up going to Mt Penang [Juvenile Justice Centre] for three months before I turned eighteen. It was alright [there], I guess. Every day we'd get up at about seven o'clock and we'd be assigned different work areas. My group had to clean toilets around [the town of] Yeoval and stuff [although] once you've been there for a while you can opt to work in the area of carpentry or dairy.

When I got out I was back on the streets, living at mates' places and squats in Sydney. At the time I was doing marijuana and speed [amphetamine]. I stayed in squats for about three or four months [but] left because it was dirty with fuckin' cockroaches and rats.

Then I went to gaol for two months for car theft again. I got caught when we were doing burnouts and the car stalled. The next thing I knew this blue and red flashing light was coming towards us. I started running and got tackled. I thought, well, I'm over eighteen now so I'm going to prison. [This time] I went to Parklea Prison. [In there] you're in lock-up most of the day. During the day you go to work, but if [there was none] we'd get sent back to the cells and just play cards all day. You could get drugs. I did some cones [of marijuana] and a couple of pills, but [Parklea] rattled me. [When I got out] I didn't do crime again. I got back into the same old scene, in and out of refuges, on the streets and in squats. Every six months I'd meet new people. They move on and you move on but you might bump into them down the track.

Todd Parker

When I was nineteen I ended up going back to the Central Coast for a while and lived with a mate [who] had a house. I lived there for about a year. Then his dad died. Well, his dad owned the place so they [the family] sold it and we couldn't live there no more. I wasn't in contact with me family and they didn't try to track me down. That was alright, I guess. I'd been on me own most of the time anyway. So I thought I'd come back to Sydney and check it out again.

I went to Foster House [men's shelter] for about three months. I wasn't doing any more crime and the [social welfare] payment covered the rent, plus I had about $200 left over every fortnight. [So] I just watched TV all day and not much [else]. After [Foster House] I went into Campbell House [men's shelter] for two months [and] read books and watched TV. I'd get bored and go for walks.

Me caseworker put me on this live-in program for about two or three months. They did piss [urine] tests every two weeks. You can't do drugs. You can drink, but you can't come back drunk and stuff. I was still smoking pot [and] one day I got pulled up and the counsellor said, 'What do you want to do? Do you want to keep on smoking [marijuana] or do you want stay in the program?' I said I wanted to keep on smoking.

The next day we were going bowling and I got on the bus [to go with them]. He [the counsellor] come out and said, 'What are you doing? You want to get out somewhere?' They kicked me out. I was pretty shocked. I thought they'd give me at least a week to decide if I was going to leave or not. After that, I went back to Foster House again for three months. While I was there I went through a paranoid psychosis from [doing] drugs, a heavy amount of speed and pot. I kept hearing voices, all different ones. I didn't know what was happening to me or where the voices were coming from. I realised they were in me head and I couldn't really explain it. At one point they [the voices in my head] were talking about plotting to kill me family. I could hear them talking about it. [The voices] weren't even in the background, so it was pretty full-on. Most of the chemicals they put in speed and pot these days make you go crazy.

When I was going through the psychosis I got the crisis team from Darlinghurst Community Health Centre's [Caritas Psychiatric Service] out two nights in a row. They gave me pills and helped me calm down a bit. But I still kept on with the pot and the speed. That lasted for three months and I slowed down [the drug use] eventually. I ended up putting meself [back] in Caritas [Psychiatric Service]. They give you pills to help you calm down and make the voices go away. I put meself in there for two days to straighten out but I got out and did drugs again. Then they got me on injections every few weeks and I got medication to take, too. I haven't taken it for a while.

Two or three years ago I went back up to Wyong and had [taken] some caps of [magic] mushrooms. For the next four or five days I went mad. I thought me landlord wanted to kill me. I went to the local cop shop and said, 'Can you help me?' They wouldn't, so I ended up sleeping on the bench outside [the police station] until six o'clock in the morning. I ended up going in there and said, 'If you're not going to take me to Mandala [Mental Health Clinic] can you give me a few bucks to get there?' So I went into Mandala for a month. They put me on pills [again]. I just went through it [the psychosis], even though it was really scary sometimes.

I've been doing ice [methamphetamine] and pot lately. I'll be getting some money soon from welfare but I don't want to touch it. It's like party time, you're thinking you can hit the bars and get drunk as a skunk and high as a kite. But I pay me rent first and this pay I want to buy new clothes. I don't want to get caught onto ice again. Last payment I was meant to pay rent but I ended up staying at a mate's place and didn't pay it. Me and me mate took $300 or $400 worth of ice in three or four days.

The worst part about ice is that you get the high and you buy stuff you don't need. You might buy more ice or you might just buy grog but the grog doesn't affect you so you just sit there drinking. That's where your money goes. I felt like shit after that. I woke up in the next couple of days and thought, 'Where did me money go?' I didn't even have enough to pay for a packet of cigarettes to get me through the next two weeks. Then I bumped into one of the workers at Darlinghurst [Community Centre's Caritas Psychiatric Service] and asked if I could come back and get me injections every two weeks and get back on the pills. I want to stop [doing] drugs because I know I'm going to go through another paranoid psychosis episode. I'm trying to quit. The pay before that I got to the point where I only bought $40 worth of pot.

Sometimes I want to see me family and me niece, me sister's daughter. I haven't seen her for a while. We're still mates [but] I'm not really in contact with me brother. I'll probably go back one day and say hello. It's hard [to go back] and see me mum. The last time

Todd Parker

I saw her she said, 'Don't come home.' I felt pretty shitty [hearing that]. Eventually I want to get back with her. When I do ring her I tell her how I've been. In Sydney there's just me dad's parents but I don't see them, I've only met them once. I'm [also] still in contact with some old friends from the Central Coast [who live in Sydney], but there's nobody [else] down here.

Living in a squat was never easy. Some sqats were cold [with] no toilets and no electricity in them. You don't get much sleep in a squat because of the cold, [so] you put as many clothes on as you can. You have to try and find mattresses, cushions and blankets. Most of the time you just sit around doing nothing.

On the streets I mostly slept on park benches for a couple of weeks at a time and I [also] used to sleep on trains; they were warm. You just get a ticket and stay on it [the train]. The police would come and get you up at about three o'clock in the morning. They'd ask, 'What are yeh doing?' I'd say, 'Trying to get some sleep. What does it look like?' They'd kick you off at the station but sometimes they'd just let you sleep.

There's a car park at the [Sydney] Entertainment Centre [and] I used to sleep there a lot. I'd go in through a gate. There was this shed and a [loose] door. I'd put the door down as a bed and sleep on that and use me sleeping bag as a blanket. I never got caught there.

[Once] I slept outside the Convention Centre in Darling Harbour. I was trying to get to sleep one night and two security guards came up and said I had to move on. They just stood there and watched me as I packed up all me gear and left. I've had no problem with the general public. I mean, I don't advertise that I'm homeless—I wear clean clothes and that. They think I'm just another person;

they don't know. Sometimes you see guys who are just filthy [and] dirty. There's a guy with his trouser legs rolled up with black feet and legs [from dirt]. If they got help they would see [the way they're living] in a different light. They probably think they have no hope in the world [or] that they're not getting the help they want. So they just go down the path they've naturally been on their whole lives.

Now I've got a place and that's the first step. I just take life as it comes. That's the way I've been living the last twelve years anyway. [These days] I go to The Station [Drop-in Centre], watch TV, read, go back home around one o'clock [in the afternoon], read, go to the food van. I can always get a meal. At eight o'clock [at night] you can go down to the food van at Hyde Park.

[Looking back] I feel like I could have done better, I should have done better. I want to become a youth worker, so I've got to go back and finish high school and then do a four-year course on youth work. They prefer you to have life experience [for youth work] but they do want the tertiary education as well. Once I get off drugs that's where I want to get to. I'd like to work in a place like Mt Penang [Juvenile Justice Centre]. But I need to cut [out using] ice completely and cut way down on the pot.

Josephine
age 43

I'm a Sydney girl. I was brought up by an Aboriginal mother from the mission, who wanted to come to Sydney to make a new life. Not under the Aboriginal Protection Board; her mission was more like a reserve for workers on the [NSW] North Coast. My dad is Sicilian. He came [to Australia] from the war and he was very poor. Of course, their diets were both poor but it didn't reflect in mine. When they married they must have subconsciously realised that food was something that they never had and they wanted us kids to have it.

Unfortunately, I was the 'us kids'. I was the only child they had so I was very spoilt. My nanna, she was a real Italian *nonna*, had a shop in Leichhardt that sold groceries, lollies and chips. Those things were abundant [in my childhood]. I suffer for it now as an adult.

Josephine

As a young woman, my parents got divorced and I was living with my dad, who was very violent. I was nineteen, straight out of school. That's why I can say I've always been kept; my family always kept me. I was kept on the Italian side so there were standards I had to live up to, which were very, very hard. The Italian side of the family was very successful because there were so many adults in the household and not a cent was squandered. When I broke away from home, from my dad, I had to stay up by myself.

Then I fell in love with this guy from Zambia, he was over here on a scholarship. This was in Brisbane. I knew a lot of the Murris up there. I had a child and I really wanted to be with the guy I loved. So I went with him to Zambia. He paid for my fare, and we started a life there in the early 1980s. Of course it was very hard; I was from a different culture. Here, [in Australia], I've got black heritage but my culture's still very different to his. He was very materialistic. I found that his ways and my ways totally conflicted.

So I came back, with a child, and I wasn't up to the expectations of the Italian side at all. I was a sort of mother because I had married but then I chose to be single again. But I knew my marriage wasn't going to last so I settled back in Sydney again. From that moment I started finding myself in situations where I was homeless.

Then my ex-husband joined me back in Australia [after] my Italian uncle, God bless him, brought him back. One day my uncle just said to me, 'So come on, let's go to the airport.' I asked why. He said, 'Your husband's arriving.'

We tried to make a go of it again. I tried so hard but he'd lost me. That was very hard. From 1985 I knew I was going to be a single mum. We tried over the years. I had seven pregnancies and only my one child with him that we were blessed with. When my son was three years old I moved around and I tried to live with family.

I found I was so different, being more Italian than Aboriginal. But I found it was easier to live with Aboriginal standards than Italian standards, because no-one on the Aboriginal side was critical of me. They didn't criticise me for anything; they loved me for who I was. Whereas with the Italian side, I had to live up to so much and it was hard because I didn't have the person I wanted to do it with.

Also, I had a Negro child. With the racism [we experienced] I found it hard to get accommodation. My very first stint with real estate, to get into a private rental, was incredible. I'd done the right thing and found myself with the real estate people eventually blacklisting me for a mark that was on the carpet. To this day I have the lease and it showed clearly that the mark and spot was already on the carpet [before I'd even rented it].

I had to live with family and was obliged to hand over all of my childcare pension, which left me with nothing, because we were living in totally over-crowded households. If someone had a Housing Commission home then there'd be seven or eight of us [living in it]. Drugs were in every frigging household. I lived in the Sydney suburbs of Mt Druitt, Petersham and the inner city; so many I can't remember them all. I also put my name down on the [NSW Department of Housing] list.

I also lived in Redfern on 'the Block'. That was wonderful. But I really stuffed up there. [At the time] the residents were going to boycott paying rent to Aboriginal Housing. Silly duffer me did that and of course I got evicted. I loved being there and cuddling the children, listening to kiddies and meeting family that I didn't know of. I'm still close to [them] to this day. The Aboriginal side of the family is very large. I think there were forty-nine cousins at one stage and there's forty-seven of them still. It was a wonderful lifestyle on 'the Block' in the early 1980s. I can't say that for these days. There were still dangers [then] but you had to be sensible and clever.

So I found myself homeless again. The last women's refuge that I lived in was at Penrith. [Then] there was the First International Indigenous Women's Conference in Adelaide in 1988. I decided to go there. Of course I fell in love [there] and never came back; well, I didn't come back for a year. When we came back we settled down with some friends again. Of course it was getting to that stage where this [staying with friends] had to stop.

Fortunately, the Department of Housing offered me a place at Bankstown. I'm grateful to the Aboriginal organisations that helped me, too. I'd lived in twenty-nine places with my son, until he was six years old. The only reason I got that house was because a doctor insisted that I be housed. The medical condition was 'homelessness'. To this day I can still remember the doctor writing 'homelessness' as my medical condition. [Seeing that written down] was wonderful, it was a breakthrough. [It was] recognition of what was causing my ill health and [the ill health of] my son as well. He was of school age and I couldn't keep shifting him around any more. [It reached a point where] he needed to settle down.

I remember when we were homeless [and my son] had a skin problem around his mouth; it was like he had ice-cream around it.

Josephine

Once we were housed it just disappeared. When we were home-less I couldn't see the problems he was suffering. I could only see what I was going through. Living in Aboriginal housing at Bankstown was good. I found myself living with multicultural people. Bankstown was starting to really draw in the Asians and the Arabic-speaking people [back then]. For me, I fitted in. I found my place.

Then, two years down the track my Italian uncle rang me and told me he was diagnosed with HIV. He was the one who'd gotten my husband back from Zambia; he also wanted to find another partner and live his own life and move on. What he said was, 'Do you want to move back to Leichhardt?' I said, 'Absolutely.' He said, 'If you do, you'll never be homeless.' I had the choice to live upstairs from the shop where I grew up, because my nanna had passed on, or to live next door, where Mary the bus driver had lived for years. My uncle said it would be better for me to move into Mary's place because she was his tenant and was looking to move out anyway. It had a back garden and I had a kid and a German shepherd. I said I'd love to.

I didn't pay full market price because my uncle really wanted to put me under his wing. This would have been when I was thirty or thirty-one because I lost my uncle when I was thirty-two. He even-tually died from an AIDS-related illness. His heart had fluid around it; his heart drowned.

That was very sad, because he was the only person who helped me in my life [like that]. Him and my nanna were really, really lovely. Before he died my uncle wanted to know why I spent so much time with the 'darkies', the darker [coloured] side of the family. Now he grew up with racism too [and] got called a wog and a spic, everything possible; but he meant it affectionately, because he loved my mum. He was a gentleman. He was no screaming queen, he was a real gentleman. I miss him.

My dad is still alive but he's not close to me. We're still in contact through my stepmother. I only had one father and mother and for all their faults I love them both. I used to pray when I was a child that they'd get back together. Then I became an adult and realised what life was all about and thank God they didn't get back together. To this day my dad [still] loves my mum.

I found that even though I was very much Italian in my ways I was also very Koori in my ways. I've always maintained contact with the Koori side and I felt that I was punished for that. Maybe it was because I couldn't conform to the Italian ways and I found myself homeless that way. When my uncle died, in his will he left the house [which we were renting] to my son and myself. We became fifty–fifty owners of our home. It was wonderful.

We've been there twelve years now. We haven't been homeless for twelve years and I hope that we don't become homeless again because we have a mortgage. [In taking out a mortgage] we weren't trying to keep up with the Joneses; it really needed to be repaired, because that house was always a rental property. I thought, I've got a son and I'm not going to live forever. He owns the home, too. I'd like to see him make a go of himself.

I work for the dole at Mac Silva Centre [Aboriginal Shelter] and my income is pretty low. I work eighteen hours a week for $192. It's better than nothing and I really love it. I'm gaining wonderful skills there. I have administration training and I haven't been able to apply those skills [until now]. That was one of the courses that I tried. It's hard to keep up with how many [I've done] or how many government departments I've bloody worked for. I really want to work back in the community.

Sometimes being homeless can be a blessing in disguise because you don't have to hand so much bloody money out! I nearly lost $2000 worth of jewellery in hock [recently]. I was so lucky that someone cared about me and got it for me. I couldn't afford to get it out on my wages. I've got bills constantly and I've got to put a little bit here and there. This is another turning point in my life. I find it a bit ironic that I was homeless all those years [then] settled for many years and now it's, 'Oh my god, we could be homeless again.' I know my son wouldn't allow that to happen. He's got a good head on his shoulders for a young black man. I'm very proud.

I didn't want to ask for charity, but unfortunately a year ago my partner left me and I really needed help. St Vincent de Paul were marvellous. I was a full-time student on a low income, trying to run a house but wanting independence [at the same time]. You really have got to become responsible. I never knew as a child that we were so lucky; I never knew what a bill was [back then]. But [now] you do without [things] because you know bills have to be paid.

I want to be responsible. I think that is what the Italian side of the family was saying: conform to our ways and you've got to live with responsibility. I think the grades show that I have done that, although sometimes the choices that I made were not necessarily good. But I was living in women's housing with a child and I was working at the time. I think [the Italian side of the family] overlooked the fact that I had a child.

When I was twenty-six I decided to go back and get an education. I mean I had gone to the best schools [when I was a kid] but school had been of no value to me to [back then]. I had a poor education as a result. I went back as an adult and I found out that going back with a child on your hip wasn't easy.

I went to Tranby [Aboriginal Cooperative College] in Glebe and sat for my Year 12 Certificate, to get into university, and I got that. Unfortunately, I found that when I was homeless in those periods I couldn't balance it. I tried so hard to be a student but I was homeless and had to work and get accommodation and care for a child. It was also hard because I was looked down upon. I think it was because I was Aboriginal, and [because] I had a Negro child on my hip and it wasn't the common sight here in Sydney. I was told once at Canterbury Hospital to make my way back to Redfern even though I was living somewhere close to the hospital itself! I was living in a squat.

Squatting was actually a really interesting lifestyle. I knew many young women who were homeless and squatting and who made wonderful homes out of it for their families. It was wonderful to see other people cooking and making homes. In that lifestyle you [voluntarily] shared with others, so it was a real collective. But I didn't live in them for very long. I'm a person who needs to have electricity and water in a home. We lived in squats for very short periods [at a time].

Josephine

I think the first time I stayed in a refuge was at the [Elsie] Women's Refuge at Glebe. They would put you up in a place and put you on the Housing Commission list. Unfortunately, it took me six years [to get Housing Commission accommodation]. It's getting longer [these days]. Living in refuges was very hard; it felt so wrong. It felt wrong to have a child in that space with other women. There was an Aboriginal hostel that got closed down not long ago. [That was] Ngura [Hostel] in Lewisham and we actually had to live there in a dormitory with women and children in the same room. Your child would have a toy and he had to share it. You had clothes and you had to share them. There was no privacy, basically. You couldn't fart.

You try to protect your child from anyone coming near them. When you live in share accommodation you don't have any control [over who is there] and you have to trust people. I remember living with so many people and wondering after, did anything happen? Fortunately, no abuse occurred.

Cultural barriers [were also a problem]. I was in a refuge one time and another resident got tense and upset [with me]. We were in the laundry and I accidentally touched her and she got violent. She didn't like me touching her. I don't know why. I think if you have women with children [in a shelter] it's more tense because women are very protective. We're terribly territorial. I've also done a lot of counselling and work in women's services and women can really sock you over. Also, when you're living in a refuge the authorities treat you as a victim. It's like, fuck, I'm a woman and I've got to empower myself. At that time, in the 1980s, the feminist movement in Sydney was just booming and you did feel you were like superwomen because you had wonderful women around you.

The circle of people I knew at the time were really tough bloody bitches and they lobbied. They lobbied the government. They just gave it to men. They made changes. This is what I find with a lot of young people who are very disrespectful [today]. I think, who the fuck are you? You have no idea how much I fought so that you would have a home. I think I went to every bloody rally in Sydney! We lived in tents in Canberra as well. We did that on the parliament lawn with one of the women's lobby groups. It was freezing, with no mattress and no blankets. That was a hard time, but it was a good experience because I knew I could deal with it.

I couldn't say that women with children have priority [to get housing]. There are still women and children living in cars. Actually, that's how I was taken off the street in Redfern. I was sleeping in a car out the front of a couple's place. They were very nice to me and ended up taking me in. They offered us a room. I loved them for that. I found out we were sort of related. When they decided to move out I was given their terrace up on Caroline Street in Redfern. Unfortunately, I found out recently that the husband had passed on.

There were a lot of implications of being homeless. Socially, it was very hard. You didn't have independence. It was very hard to get any help from welfare because they want you to have a permanent address and I couldn't give one. But when I was housed, welfare helped tremendously.

Josephine

Being homeless wasn't just about me; it was about my child as well. He was my life and I wanted him to have better [opportunities]. He was my first priority and he helped me a lot, too. And no matter what, whether it was drugs or alcohol, I never gave him up. I'm so lucky I never lost him to welfare [Department of Community Services]. The pub was next to my college and there was a Children's Court next door. We were allowed to have children in the bar. But I remember [one day] welfare people were drinking there and one of them threatened me. It frightened the fuck out of me. They have a lot of power.

I don't think the government is responsible enough [with homelessness and its causes]. You have a lot of public servants, and these people are a breed of their own. They're just like a process line, and the big issues rarely get to the big people, but they should know [what's going on]. At election time [solutions and incentives] come up and they're just a bullshit thing to get the votes. There's not much done. I'd like to see people lobby their local government, their local council. Local government might [provide] more help than higher levels of government.

Being homeless was a very draining experience and I wouldn't recommend it to anyone. I still have family, young nieces and nephews, that want to move out of home but they're just not financially stable. It's just not easy to get on the dole or to get a job. All I say to them is, 'Stay at home. Communicate a bit better with your parents and family. Don't have such a grudge on your shoulders.' I find that homelessness for me started from [my childhood] home, so I think there has to be more communication there. Unfortunately, they [my nieces and nephews] remind me of me, and that's why I don't want that happening for them. It's not worth it. They can get mixed up with the wrong people and I don't want that. Homelessness can lead to crime. I'm no angel. I've done things that I'm not pleased about, but I had to survive.

When it comes to teenagers I find I come from another planet. I've got a lot of love for young people but I just don't understand them. They're so fucking different [in] the way they speak; they've got such a lack of respect. It's really frightening. I feel that we are assimilating too much into white society. I don't want to see that. I don't want a blackfella to be a whitefella; I want a blackfella to be a blackfella.

The youth have got all the social things to get through, all the peer pressure. There's the drugs. Cocaine is so available in Leichhardt, and then, the Harry [heroin] and crack is a big thing. When my son was younger I always used to think, what the hell is he going to be up against? What drug will he be tempted with? I don't even know what they [drugs] are called half the time. I'm just happy my son is at the age he is now, twenty-one. I'm glad he developed as an individual, into an adult, quickly.

I found that when I was homeless I was very tough; I wouldn't let many people stand over me. Unfortunately, with your own family it's different because of the emotional ties. I think I learned a lot and I often wonder how I survived it [homelessness]. I don't know whether it was my make-up, sheer luck, or all of the above. I'm very religious in my ways. I have my own faith and I was brought up with Catholicism for the early part of my life. I know what I feel comfortable with. I find I still say my Hail Marys and Our Fathers. I just go outside and say a few things and thank someone because I feel that I am fortunate. I don't want to feel a victim of my own life. I want to move on.

I think people just have to empower themselves, more than anything. If you've gone beyond prevention [you need to] ask for help. Don't be shy and scared and sit down and wait for the help. Ask people for help, because being homeless is no joke; it is a really draining experience.

Jay
age 22

The names of people in this chapter are not their real names.

I've left home and gone back twelve or more times since I was sixteen. My mum and dad have always taken me back, so when I was in strife I could go back. The first time I left home was in Year 8. I stayed with a friend of mine for a few weeks. This time I've been out of home for twelve months now. As I got older I went further away [from home] each time. I've probably done the whole train line—that was a bit of fun.

I have a younger brother and sister. I've only just learnt that I've been so jealous and so nasty to my sister. I'd always felt that she and my brother were better than me. My brother played sport, my sister went through to Year 12 and I turned out to be the bum. It just made me real mad. I can't go to visit my mum or dad without fighting with my sister.

Jay

It all started, I think, around sixteen [years of age] when I got into weed [marijuana] and then I got really heavily into alcohol. It began with the weed but I built up a tolerance after a while and bourbon lasted longer. Well [at least] you think it does. In Year 10 I was drinking and I was being sent home from school all the time because I was turning up drunk. I was becoming very aggressive. My mum would be picking me up from school because I was getting kicked out for throwing a table out the window. At one stage, when I was living with Mum and Dad I started stealing money and things from the house to pay for my speed [amphetamine], drink and cigarettes. That started when I was around fifteen but it kept on going until I was eighteen.

I think what really got me started [running away from home] was this: I have epilepsy and my mum is very over-protective. She has to know everything and see everything and all this bullshit. The other thing is my mum let my sister grow up a lot quicker than me because I think they think more of her than they do of me. That all started to get too much for me and I needed my space. I didn't need people to look after me. My mum was looking after my epilepsy medication for me day and night. I was like, 'Mum, I can do it', but she wouldn't have it. If I live with them I have to hand over all my medication. Even right now, my mother will ring me where I'm living and all she has to say is, 'Have you been taking your medication? Have you had any seizures?' I don't think she realises that I've grown up. I'm a big boy and a lot more happens than that sort of shit.

My mum was always into stopping me from using chemical drugs like speed and stuff because of my epilepsy. But I think it

Above: Davo Marsh, a poet and a man with a deep understanding of street spirituality.

Left: Davina Coad spends each day speaking with other homeless people offering compassion, advice and an open heart.

Above:
'The government
needs a bloody kick
up the arse ... Take a
look at what's going
on all overAustralia.'
— Mike Reeves

Right: 'It was
absolutely scary
when I first started
sleeping rough. I see
some people on their
first day and they
look horrified.'
— Henry

Above: A homeless woman feeding the birds in Hyde Park in the afternoon sun.

Right: Looking like abandoned bags of rubbish, many streeties stash their possessions and blankets away for the day, returning to set up camp at night. As this shot was being taken, three young men squatted at a wall shooting up heroin. They weren't keen to be photographed.

Above: 'There are still women and children living in cars. Actually, that's how I was taken off the street in Redfern. I was sleeping in a car out the front of a couple's place who where very nice to me and ended up taking me in.' — Josephine

Below: Although this is probably the most common aspect of homelessness the public sees, it is not indicative of the entire homeless community. This man had been drinking heavily on a hot afternoon and had fallen asleep where he sat.

Above: A homeless woman's 'home' at Circular Quay.

Right: Clients of
The Station Ltd catch
afternoon TV and coffee
in the upstairs café.
For many it's a welcome
chance to be off the
streets for a few hours.

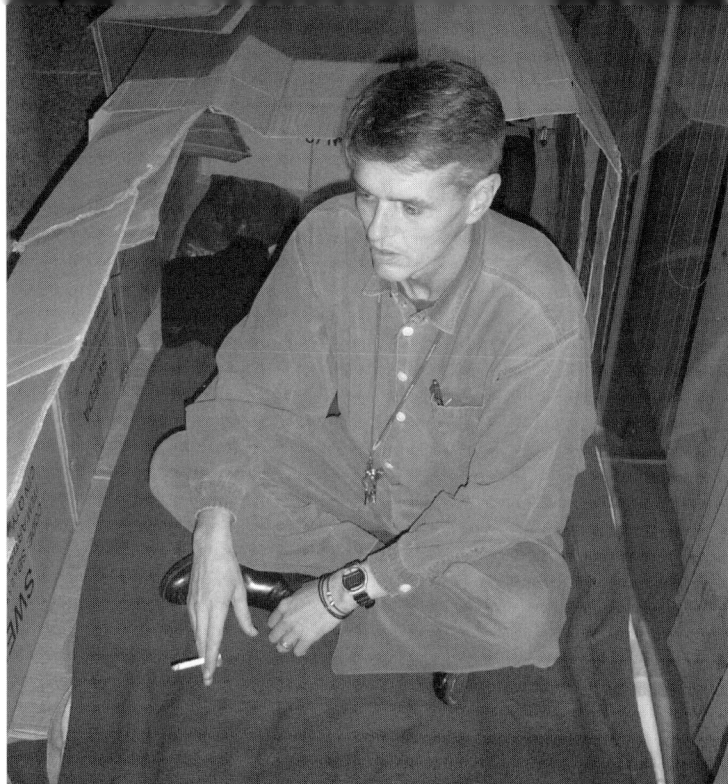

Above: 'It's a joke among the different people that know me and have seen where I sleep.' — John 'the architect' can build a shelter out of nothing but a handful of cardboard. Pictured here behind the State Library.

Right: 'Looking back I see it as like going surfing, catching a wave and going through a tube. It's all darkness around you in a big tunnel and you see the light at the end. I finally got spat out the other side, above the wave.'—Ray

Above: 'Mirror Boy'; artwork by Liam.

Below: Nathan at a building site in the city where he slept at night.

Left: 'I wouldn't walk down the street all ratty-tatty and torn [but] who cares if someone has a hole in their shirt. You just don't look down on them—they're people as well.' — Linz

Below: Sleeping bag and blanket abandoned at the edge of Hyde Park, across from St Mary's Cathedral, Sydney.

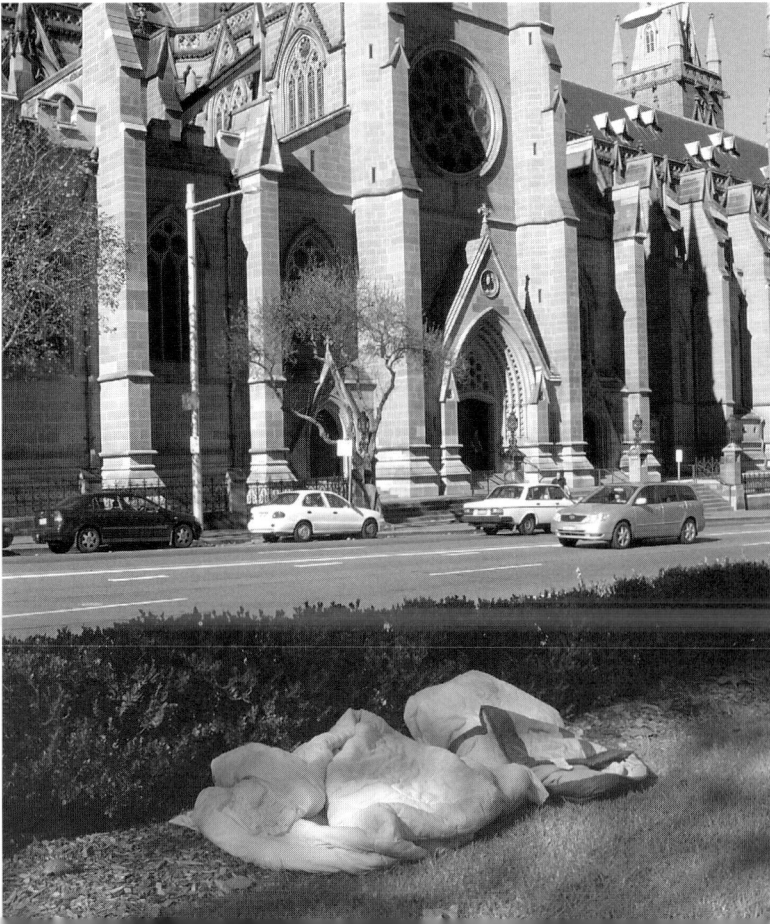

Jay

was Dad who stopped me doing both the drinking and speed in the end. He sat me down and said, 'That's it.' At the time I was getting really cranky, so they locked me in the backyard for a while until I settled down. Then they looked out the bathroom window asking, 'Are you okay to come back in the house then?' I was wearing myself out going mad out there. Since then I haven't touched anything other than pot.

That last time I went home [twelve months ago] my dad wrote out a sheet of rules because, as usual, I was drinking too much and smoking too much weed, coming home and waking up the whole family when I came in. So one day my dad said, 'Tomorrow, you're going to have a list on the table, a list of rules. If you don't want to follow these rules leave your keys on the table.' He wanted me to sign it to say I agreed. I looked at it and didn't sign. I didn't like the rules. So I put my keys on the table. It was getting late so I thought I'd just crash for the night and leave in the morning but he wouldn't let me do that. I had to leave right then.

Anyway, I finished Year 10 and ran away again during Year 11 and just decided, nah, bugger it. I'd spent the previous few years outside the bloody principal's office and I'd been kicked out of school so much that I'd missed [my studies] anyway.

I used to have a drink [of alcohol] at the shops across the road at about ten o'clock in the morning, go to school and smoke weed in the toilets. Teachers didn't like me and I didn't like them. It got to the stage with my friends where they weren't inviting me to parties because they were worried that I'd start drinking and get out of control. I only found that out a couple of years ago.

Jay

When I was eighteen, there was this neighbour, Melanie, who lived across the street from our house. One day I had a fight with Mum and I grabbed me bag and dragged it across the street [to Melanie's house] and I lived there for a little while. [At the time] I also had a girlfriend, Becky, [and] she moved into Melanie's with me. We [Becky and I] had a fight because I was cheating on her with a guy. We were supposed to share our bed but she went to the guy next door and started rooting him to rub it in. So I had to sleep on the couch and occasionally I'd hear someone else with my girl-friend. That drove me up the wall. When it was all over she said, 'I only did it to bloody get back at you.' Well it worked.

Each time I left home I'd return because I ran out of money or I couldn't find someone to stay with. Because of my epilepsy I also get the DSP (Disability Support Pension). I also got money from working at a coat-checking place and selling drugs from there. I was the runner for a drug seller and that was busy, especially on Friday and Saturday nights.

Also, I had two friends who were working 'the wall' [a street prostitution spot in Sydney] and they were always going on about how much money they made. In 2002, I worked 'the wall' and did a bit of prostitution. It wasn't really a decision I made; I had to do it to get money to survive. But it was really embarrassing. The first time I actually did it was to pay for a cab fare to get home. Sometimes it would make me cry because you just feel so bad.

When I've been homeless I've also gone and met men in bars just to get somewhere to spend a night. One night I met this guy, Ben. He drove me home the next day and I packed my bags and told my mum and dad, 'I'm going to Bathurst.' So I lived with him in

Jay

Bathurst for a month until his rental lease ran out and we had nowhere to go. We went to a backpackers hostel but we just didn't have the money to continue so I went to see another guy I knew called Alex, who lives in Kogarah, and sort of handed myself over to him for a place to stay. I had to do that, have sex with him, to keep a roof over my head. I mean, I had my boyfriend, Ben, but I was out of choices.

It was one of the most degrading things I've ever done but it was the situation I was in. Ben couldn't handle it and he didn't stay long. We haven't spoken since. Alex, who was five years older than me, was happy to settle down and stuff and I wasn't so I left there in a hurry.

My parents knew I was living with a gay guy [Alex] and they never rang me in that whole time. My brother was the only one who rang me then. My parents knew I was bisexual. One day last year they came home and caught me with a male backpacker. I dressed him and I got dressed myself and went in and introduced him to my father. My mum just doesn't understand the whole bisexuality thing. For her it's either one or the other. When I came out and told them my dad couldn't even look me in the eye. I could play pool and have a drink of bourbon with him and even during that he'd only say things like, 'Good shot.' There was no conversation at all.

[Recently] I met up with my family when my sister was moving to Queensland. At the airport we were sitting around eating pizza and it was so hard for me to talk to my dad. The only person I could speak to was my brother. My dad was more interested in the news and sport on the television which was over my shoulder. I think that's really sad.

Jay

When I first started leaving home it wasn't hard to find a place to stay because I had a lot of friends around [the suburb I lived in]. But when I went to Bathurst and came back after a month everybody had finished Year 12 and just disappeared. [People's] mobile phone numbers no longer existed or they'd moved out of their homes. I'd come back and everyone was gone. It was a bit of a shock.

The [most recent] period of time I've been out of home went so quickly. The last time I went home my little brother, who is sixteen now, had grown to [be] six foot three. He was huge and had facial hair! I thought, where have I been? I go to Mum and Dad's on the weekends if I've got the money. There's still that friction between myself and my sister. Every time I go there she'll be screaming, 'What the hell are you doing coming back here and causing all this trouble?' That brings me close to tears.

I slept in Hyde Park one night and walked up along Oxford Street the next day because that's where I could try and get picked up or get some money. I saw a sign for the Come in Youth Resource Centre [run by St Francis Welfare] and walked in. I was lucky because they got me into Foster House [men's shelter] and then into St Laurence House [which offers] a semi-independent housing program [for homeless youth]. My flatmates constantly stole stuff like CDs from me just to get money. So I moved out of there and now I'm in a new place that is so much better. I pay a small rent, about $45 [a week] but don't have to pay for gas or electricity.

My grandmother used to say, 'After all wrong there comes a good.' Well, now I've done all my wrongs. I'm proud of where I am now, but I've had to learn it all the hard way. With all that I've been through I was able to learn a lot early [in life] and now I've got hope. I'm over chemical drugs you can't be sure what's in them anyway. With weed, it's sweet [okay]; it comes off of a plant! I was with someone the other day and said, 'I can smell pot.' And they replied, 'I think you sweat it!'

As I said, the last time I went home my brother had grown up a lot. One of the things that connected us most was cigarettes and alcohol, because he's in high school and he's partying now. Now I've got that little bit of wisdom and I can sit down with him and have a chat about things like that, unlike Mum and Dad. I'm able to tell him a lot. I see myself in him and I feel concerned because I can see him following down my path, with him taking all these pills and alcohol. You find that when they tell you something at school [about drugs and alcohol] that it's not really like they say it is. They fill your brain with all that shit. All those years that I was sitting around that table [at school] and I would think, I'm not listening because you have no idea how it really is.

Over the next few years I'm going to try and write a book. I used to have to carry around a pen because I'd have an idea and need to write it down. I have just been registered to go to school again. It's just that bit of motivation that I need. I get up in the morning and I put me bloody best rags on and a nice shiny pair of shoes. They say, 'Where are you going?'

I say, 'Nowhere.' But to get up and dress nice and do your hair nice [makes] you feel good. You are able to get up and know that today is another day even if you're only hanging around the house doing the vacuuming.

Jay

Because one of my flatmates has a job at KFC and I'm still waiting to re-enter school I end up [doing] the cleaning and sit around waiting for the Department of Housing to come around and fix windows and shit like that. So I'm like, 'You tell me I don't have a job? I'm the bloody receptionist, cleaner, worker; I do it all.' I'm starting to become a housewife! My mum brought us up so that we have always done our own washing and cleaning so I knew that sort of stuff when I left home. But it never seemed that important at Mum and Dad's. But when you come in and you go, 'Yeah, this is my couch, this is my kitchen' you think, oh my God! It looks like a bomb's hit it. How can I live in this? I never noticed when Mum and Dad were bitching about it.

Jai

age 25

I was brought up in country South Australia. I spent all of my high school years there. When I was very young my parents got divorced. Then in my final year of high school I had a nervous breakdown from a lot of unresolved problems in the family. So I didn't end up getting my HSC [Higher School Certificate], which was really difficult for me. After that I decided to live back in Adelaide rather than in the country. The government wouldn't give me money to live independently so I had to try to prove that I couldn't live with either of my parents. I was about eighteen.

I had to live with my dad. It was a very hard time because I don't have a very good relationship with my dad. I have lots of problems with him from the past, a bit of violence and things like that. So I decided to live with my dad for six months to prove that I couldn't live with him. It doesn't make a lot of sense, but that's what I did.

Jai

It finally got to a point where I left home. My dad calls it running away from home, but I don't think I was running away. I think I was going somewhere better. That was my first experience of being homeless. I went to a refuge for young women in Adelaide. There's only one youth refuge for women [in Adelaide] and two for young guys. There's no refuges for women over twenty-five [years of age] unless they're experiencing domestic violence. I was lucky I was still young so I could go to the youth refuge.

That was the beginning of the cycle of homelessness for me. From there I went into supported housing and I actually went backwards in the system. I went from [an] outreach [program] into twenty-four-hour support. Because I've got mental health issues they felt I needed more support. [At the time] my case manager was sick, so decisions were made without her knowledge or my consultation. They didn't say, 'Jai, what do you think would be the best thing to do?' They went ahead and put me into twenty-four-hour support.

Then I got asked to leave because of some stuff that I did while I was living there, some pretty wild and dangerous stuff. I got taken into hospital with my mental health issues. While I was there I was told that I couldn't live at the refuge, which left me homeless and living in the hospital. I stayed there for a few weeks and then I think I stayed with my cousins for a while. That was awkward, as I'm not very good at sharing my space. I like my private space a lot and so I find it really difficult to live with other people.

My mental health issues started when I was fourteen, depression and stuff like that. My first trip to hospital was when I was seventeen. I spent three months [there and] that's why I didn't do my

Jai

HSC. I knew I needed to talk to someone and I rang all the people I knew that I thought might be able to help, [like] teachers and friends, but they weren't available.

In a country town I actually found myself walking the streets, going to churches, and eventually I walked into DOCS [Department of Community Services]. I was crying and must have looked shocking, because they immediately helped me, which was really, really good of them. I still don't know to this day what made them think I was suicidal. I was, but I don't think I told them. They made me sign a contract saying I wouldn't harm myself. I don't know, but I think it was just about their safety, so they could save their arse if I tried something.

That's sort of when the mental health stuff became an obvious problem. I'd had problems when I was younger but nobody really did anything about it. And because I went to a Catholic school there were no counsellors; we were expected to talk to a priest. Yeah, a young girl talking to a priest about violence and stuff like that ... it's not really a common thing!

Because of the type of mental illness I've got I actually had some really good times. I've been overseas, twice to the Philippines to do youth work and attend international youth conferences, and [I also] helped facilitate workshops and group meetings of about a hundred people. That was through the Australian Youth Foundation, working with youth, government and society [towards] social cohesion.

The first [trip] was an exchange to do youth work. They chose six young people from Australia who had experienced homelessness to go and work with homeless people in the Philippines and then they came over to Australia [to do the same]. It was so amazing. It was good for me, being Asian myself. I'm from Thailand, not the Philippines, but I really felt that sense of belonging. There's an Asian quality, [a] sensitiveness, open and honest, [and] I just really felt like I belonged. A part of me was, not sarcastic, but cheeky. Sort of, ha-ha, I'm in the majority now, you white folks can and suffer the racism [for a change].

I worked with girls who'd been sexually abused, which was really hard work for me. I heard lots of stories from the girls that came along. There was one girl called Mikey very early in the program, and another girl called Annalin. She was in the program for the second time, which in itself was disappointing. Another girl left the program while I was there. When Annalin first came to the program she was very much like Mikey—very angry, very upset and very confused.

It was really good to see that there are programs in other countries that work in similar ways. There are obvious cultural differences. Over there, being a Catholic country, particularly for the boys' home, if you don't follow all the strict Catholic 'do's and don'ts' you aren't accepted into the program. [The] things [were] like going to confession, going to church every Sunday, praying three times a day. The boys have to make the decision: Do I do all that and get a bed and food and maybe an education, or lose out? It's harder for women because the issues that they come up [against] are harder than the men's issues. Not just for things like domestic violence, but there's a lot of sexual abuse. Prostitution is huge.

Going there just opened my eyes to the world [and] the size of the human issue. It's not just here in Sydney. It's not just in

Jai

Adelaide. It's not just in Australia. It's a world thing. It cuts across culture. It cuts across gender. It cuts across class and age and everything. Sometimes I have to remind myself that I'm not alone.

It's not selfishness, but people often wonder, why me? Sometimes it's okay spending a bit of time thinking it's dreadful but then you've got to get back to reality. And the reality is that the statistics [of homelessness and its causes] are so damn high. It's like, what are you complaining about? There's that song that goes, 'What about me? It isn't fair.' Will you just get over it? Life isn't fair. Life sucks, get on with it!

[The youth work in the Philippines] was during 1998 and 1999, after I'd moved out of my cousin's place. In Adelaide they've got a government housing system where they've got this program. Young people under twenty-five are given priority. It's not like [Sydney], where you apply for priority and everyone gets the same priority. So I managed to get housing through there and I gave it up to come to Sydney.

Sometimes I regret [moving to Sydney] and sometimes I don't. My family has always been a source of stress for me. Where I was living [in Adelaide] was on the same bus line as my dad, so I was avoiding public transport. I wouldn't go shopping where he was going shopping in case I'd see him and stuff like that. It was really quite difficult for me to live there. My mum, as much as she loves me, probably put a bit too much pressure on me as well. [She wanted me] to do better and move on with my life, in a direction that she wanted, rather than what I wanted.

Jai

While I had the government housing I managed to get a pet dog. He was the best company I'd had in a long time. I miss my dog. I don't have him any more. If I'd thought about it when I moved to Sydney I could have brought him with me. We had to take him back to the pound [because] there was nowhere else for him.

I made the decision to move [from Adelaide] on Good Friday. On Saturday I decided it was to Sydney. On Sunday I booked the tickets. On Monday I paid for the tickets. On Tuesday I hopped on the bus. Wednesday I arrived. I mean I was mentally quite unwell when I made the decision. Once I got to Sydney, though, I knew I wanted to make it work.

I've worked really, really hard to make Sydney a good place for me; to make it a place where I've got friends and support. And it's worked. I mean, it's been a very long haul. It's been three years since I moved here. Only now am I just starting to settle in terms of permanent housing, relationships with friends [and] the church life that I have. I still have nights when I don't want to be at home and I'll sleep outdoors so I feel safer.

I mean, particularly in Kings Cross, there's always someone around, and I do get lonely. I need a balance of knowledge that there are people around me, but they're not in my space. So I'd rather walk the streets at night than sit at home with really bad anxiety. The room [only] amplifies it; another hour gone [and] another hour ...

Sometimes I sleep in the inner city, but generally I hang around in Kings Cross, at the Wayside Chapel [Drop-in Centre]. A few people sleep there. You're not allowed to but people do it anyway. I don't go to Matthew Talbot [Hostel], because that's a very dangerous place for a young woman. Within the Wayside Chapel and the Rough Edges [Community Centre] I'm very well known. I know I've got protection there, but I don't have protection at Matthew Talbot so I don't go that way.

One night when I was doing really bad, there was this guy called Radio John. He's chronically homeless and mentally unstable. It's very rare when he's well enough to see outside himself, but one night he sat with me in McDonald's or somewhere in Kings Cross until two o'clock in the morning. He kept on saying, 'Jai, what's wrong? Talk to me. I know you're not well. You can trust me. You're my sister.' Then he reeled off all these people he knew I should call. The support that he gave me was amazing. Whatever was going on inside his head, he could actually see my side of things. By two o'clock he said, 'I'm goin' now.' That was fine, because from two o'clock to six o'clock I had less than four hours until something [like a support centre] opened up. He sat with me the whole time. He did the best he could and that really touched me.

I'm just amazed by the way people look out for each other on the streets. It's not always that idea of, if someone comes after you let me know and I'll bump them. That's a very masculine thing to do. But sometimes I might actually ask someone to talk to the person giving me hassle. You know, just [for someone to] let them know I'm not ignoring them but that I'm just having a hard time. That's my approach.

Alcoholic homeless people gravitate towards other alcoholic homeless people. I gravitate towards depressed people, emotional people. It doesn't always include people with depression. Often, though, I have a very strong connection with working with [the mentally ill] as well as having the experience of having a mental illness myself.

Just recently I went back to Adelaide to visit my family because my brother has problems. I didn't want to be rude to Mum but I kept on saying, 'Reality check, Mum; you are not alone. How many people are single parents? How many working mums? How many people have adopted children? Foster care? [What about] all of those statistics?'

She said, 'Yes, but what about me?' I told her, 'You are not alone'. She kept expressing her helplessness. My brother kept saying, 'You don't understand.' I said, 'Well no, I don't understand you. Everybody's depression, everybody's mental illness is different.' We can all be told that a rubbish bin is green. But you might see it as lime green. I might see it as olive green. Someone else might see it as heritage green. But the bin is green, regardless.

In narrative therapy they talk about multiple realities, that we all have our own truth. Like the green bin, my truth is valid to me and your truth is valid to you and they're still [both] true. Just because our stories are different it doesn't mean they're not valid. I found it difficult [to explain it] to my brother. It was very difficult for him to listen to what I was saying because I've been dealing with my issues for ten years [and he's only started healing].

When I [first] arrived in Sydney I got off the bus and thought, shit! I'm in Sydney. Where do I go? I had no idea where I needed to go. I hadn't planned that far ahead. My thinking, when I first got to Sydney, was that I've got to find a social worker. I didn't know where I'd find a community health centre. I didn't think of a church, because it would have been a great place to go. Churches, even if they can't give support, at least know where you can go for help.

So I ended up going to a hospital, St Vincent's Hospital. I went to the social work department and they referred me to Darlinghurst Community Health Centre. They neglected to say it was the Darlinghurst Community Centre's Caritas Pyschiatric Service. When I got there they immediately sussed me out and me, being very cagey at the time about not wanting anybody to know anything, didn't give them any information. I just gave them my name and date of birth.

They immediately saw me as a psych client. I kept on saying, 'All I need is a bed for the night. I just need a place to stay.' They wanted to know my whole story. I just wanted a place to stay! That was my first experience with Darlinghurst Community Mental Health. They found me a place for the night and talked me into leaving my stuff where it would be safe.

I don't remember the guy [counsellor] telling me to ring him to let him know I was safe. Apparently, that was what I was supposed to do and I didn't do it. So he went through all my belongings. I went right off my nut when I found out. He found the business card of my doctor in Adelaide. I found out when I called her a few weeks later that he'd called and asked if she knew me. She said, 'Yes I do [know her]. Is this a life or death situation?' He said, 'Oh, no. It's just we've seen her at the mental health centre.' She said to him, 'Well I can't give out any information on her.' I thought, you go, girl! My GP is such an amazing woman. I wrote her a letter and told her that was so excellent of her. I mean, who cares if I was depressed. That's not why I'd gone there. Maybe the next day I might have gone there for depression, but that's me asking for assistance.

My last experience with them was a few days ago. I saw a nurse and she said, 'Jai, you've changed in three years. You may still have the same problems but you think about them.' I'm like, 'Yeah, I find the same myself.' So many of those workers treat me like I was three years ago, but she was about the only person not to.

I had a time when I'd overdosed on alcohol and medication, pain-killers, everything I could find. I must have been pretty sick because I don't remember my housing support worker coming to visit. Somehow I got to the hospital and I woke up thinking, what's going on? Then they were giving me all these pills. I'm pretty cluey about pills because I've been on so many and I can recognise most of them. But there were lots of others I didn't recognise. I asked them, 'What's that? What's this one?' They were all these vitamin pills and they were saying that because I'd drunk that much alcohol [with the pills] I had an alcohol problem!

I don't drink much now. It is one of my weaknesses: if I start I'm not going to stop, and that's not a good sign. And that's [the same] with other drugs. Particularly over the past while I've been quite depressed [and] been really craving dope and Valium. The thing is, when you're under the influence of drugs [social services] people will help you. But if you want to prevent yourself from getting under the influence they won't help. There's no funding for pre-emptive help. It's like this: you've got an action and a reaction. But there are not enough facilities to pre-empt [help] so they've got to wait for the action, which is done by the client, and *then* they react.

Jai

A lot of people when they have an incident they get medicated, mended with a bandaid. The [social services professionals] don't say, 'Don't run around with scissors on a slippery floor, you might fall over.' They essentially just say, 'Bye-bye!' They don't educate you on what might happen. Funding is the big problem and early prevention is needed. [When people get into] drugs or gambling, [their addictions] are the consequences of a core [personal] issue.

I guess I became stabilised when I was with [a mental health service] in Redfern. I've got a good management plan; I just don't know how to implement it. It's just the lack of beds and lack of funding, really practical stuff, that gets in the way. Like, I tried to go to hospital recently and the only psychiatric beds that were available were in Orange and Wagga Wagga. So I went home and went through [the episode] by myself.

[In an episode like that] what goes through my mind is death and suicide. Last Monday I ran in front of a car. I've got a lovely little bruise but I didn't break any bones. I get very anxious. Anxiety often leads to psychosis for me, which is quite scary. So I try and be around what I call 'safe people', those who are reliable and knowledgeable. Like, if I'm confused with psychosis, I can ask them, 'Is there really a plant sitting on that chair?' I know that they're not going to laugh at me [but will] say, 'No Jai, you're seeing things.' Things like that.

Right at the moment I'm having a very hard time. [Recently] I've been in five different hospitals over two weeks. Going back to Adelaide was the big trigger for me. I've only been in my place for about twelve weeks, and of that I spent ten days in Adelaide, so I still haven't fully settled. I've got no furniture. Once I come out of this current depression I'll get right back into gear. I'll stabilise a lot more and make my place feel like home. When it feels like home, I'll feel much more like staying there. To walk around with a backpack on your back, and that's all you've got, is dislocating. It's really unsettling.

It can be dangerous for young homeless people, particularly for women, because that's when they get into prostitution. They often find they're depressed or lonely and they want to fall in love so they find an older man. Often the older man can be ten or twenty years older and [the girl] enters into a really unstable relationship. That often leads the girl into drugs. If you have a sixteen-year-old girl going out with twenty-eight-year-old man, that man may have been on the streets for ten years and she's only just got on the streets. He's using heroin and she's new, so he could say, 'Go sell your body for a shot [of heroin] and I'll give you a taste.' So she gets a taste for it and then gets a habit, stuff like that.

With everybody [on the streets] it's multiple issues, it's not just about being homeless. If we have to catch it [homelessness] early, then the programs need to be in schools. There is a national program called Reconnect [run by the Department of Family and Community Services] aimed at teenagers at risk of homelessness. It's a good program but nothing's ever funded enough. That's the earliest intervention I could predict. Get it before it gets to mental illness, drug-induced mental illness, alcohol or prostitution.

I think mental illness is often a trigger for homelessness, because when people get unwell other people often intrude on their lives. They say, 'You're unwell, I must look after you.' And that's often the last thing that they want. They don't want people in their face twenty-four hours a day. Because they're so unwell they run away.

That's the one good thing that Caritas [Psychiatric Service] do. They support homeless people with a mental illness by getting them somewhere to live. I think every [homeless welfare service] needs to be multi-disciplined in every social service area. Mission Australia has its own mission statement and so does The Salvation Army. I think they should try to focus [on certain aspects of homelessness] but I don't think they should ever cut off other services as a result.

If you look at the inner-city services [like] Anglicare, St Vincent de Paul, The Salvos [The Salvation Army] and Wesley Mission, there are very few services. There's maybe one or two of each of [those groups] in the city centre. What happens if St Vinnies focus on one thing and Mission Australia focus on something else? What happens if Mission Australia can't help you? You won't be able to go to another group like The Salvos because they're not funded to focus on that [particular] area.

There's a service called The Crossing [run by St Francis Welfare], which is a long-term youth case management program. All they do is case management. They don't do counselling, housing or any of those individual things. They act as coordinators for other social services. Like, I have someone from The Salvos, someone from Wayside Chapel and then I have my psychiatrist and another social worker. I've got five social workers with a case manager who keeps all of them in touch with what's happening. For example, if

Jai

I'm in hospital, she [my case manager] can tell a housing worker not to come and visit me [at home] because I'm in hospital. The Crossing is good like that. But the different services [out there] need to coordinate more.

I'm a volunteer at Rough Edges [Community Centre]. Rough Edges is so unique because the boundaries of professionalism, friendship and social support are blurred. There is a community feel. At the moment I'm actually staying at the community house run by St John [the Evangelist Church] where people can live.

Being a volunteer [at Rough Edges] is hard for me because a lot of people know that I'm quite a strong, resilient person. [But] it's hard for some people to see me when I'm unwell and to give me the space. Like, they'll come running up and go, 'Jai! Jai! Guess what, I'm pregnant. I don't know what to do!' But I can't listen to them at that time. It's hard when people don't understand. I do care, I really do. I do give time to people.

Ultimately, I want to become a psychologist and practise creative art therapy using visual and textual art, movement, music, all of those different sensory areas. I'm into talk therapy as well, but I want there to be the option if someone wants to sit and draw for half an hour and [then] say, 'I hate this picture because ... ' I'd also like to do a music course at the art centre I go to, and continue my art course in drawing. [For psychology] I need to get my HSC [NSW Higher School Certificate] and do a TAFE or university bridging course. That's the next step. At uni I'd have to do six years of full time study. I've got to think about it, [because] by then I'll be over thirty and I might want children, a family. I don't expect to stop studying until I'm about forty.

Chris Strauss
age 22

My family sort of took a trip around Australia [but] I was born in Adelaide. I was school-hopping, going [between] different towns and state to state. I mainly grew up in the Sydney area. I got brought up travelling so I can't stay in one place too long. When I went to school I had a good time. I got picked on a bit, but I picked on a few people meself. I want to get back to Adelaide [eventually]. I haven't been there since I was kid. I enjoy Queensland too much, so every time I get some money I go up there.

I have two sisters—one died—and I also have two other brothers. One brother is from the same parents. The other brother and other sister is the same mother but different father. I haven't seen me grandmother in a couple of years; time passes by and you become more distant.

Chris Strauss

From a young age Dad said [to us] that you've got to learn to fend for yourself, so ever since I was fourteen or fifteen I've always fended for meself. I've struggled and gotten back on my feet. Then, for some reason, I don't know why or how, it just eventuates into this situation [being homeless]. You have your good patches and your bad patches. Sometimes if you leave it too long the grass gets long and you get locked [into your situation]. Eventually you have to get the lawnmower out and give it a trim, you know.

After me parents split up I came down here [to Sydney from Queensland] to live with me dad. Mum came down because she missed me, so I moved back in with Mum. Then Dad started hassling Mum so she packed up. I came home from school one day when I was fourteen and only my stuff was still left in the caravan. I didn't want to go back to me dad because he got violent after a while, so I stayed around on me own. Nothing was good enough for me dad. If you didn't do it right you got a flogging and [would have to] go back again and make sure it's right.

With me mum you could have a break [or] go and have something to eat and go back and take your time. [Her attitude was], who cares if it's not right? We'll fix it up together. Then the old man comes home and, whack! [You had to] pull it apart and start again. [He'd say], 'Finish your homework, go out and work on the car and learn something educational', all this bullshit. Then I went from learning mechanics to livestock. You've got to know everything. I learned to drive horses in NSW. Then me dad got into greyhounds and I learned a bit about the greyhound scene. He used to take us to the trots [too]. If we'd go up and ask him for money for an ice-cream he'd say, 'If you can pick a winner in this race you can get a couple of bucks.' If it won he was happy, if it didn't he'd still give us a couple of bucks. Me and me brother used to [collect] $40 or $50 in cans at the horse track and that was our pocket money for a while. That was our luxury.

Me parents did the best they could, they just had problems. [After Mum left] I stayed with my best friend's family. We're still friends [now] and I'm in more contact with them than me own family. I got a job and went back to school, then dropped out in Year 10 and got a job in house building. Then I went on a roll and went to TAFE and finished me last two years [of school] in a year. I was happy, but I thought, what's an HSC [Higher School Certificate] score? It's only a piece of paper with numbers.

I had jobs. I was working for two years. I had a job in a pub in Queensland. Then I came back down here [to Sydney] and helped a friend out. They got on drugs and did the wrong thing by me and I lost me place and I couldn't sleep and couldn't get to work on time. So I lost me job. Then I was sleeping in me car. [One time] I rolled over [while asleep] and accidentally kicked the handbrake off and it crashed into some other car. I had to pay money for that. So I started having to sleep on the streets.

I thought I'd go lead me own life. I find it difficult sometimes. Like, the other day I found $10 on the street so I went and bought a pack of cigarettes and then I realised I needed $10 for rent [at temporary accommodation] so what did I buy cigarettes for? But if I didn't buy cigarettes I would've been stressing. And if you [have to] ask two guys walking up the street for a cigarette they make you feel small. If you ask half of these rich people for the time they'll not even acknowledge that you're there. I mean, how rude!

Chris Strauss

They think [that] if you're living on the streets you've got no education, that you're worthless, you're nothing, no good. I could [easily] say to them, 'You're [just] wearing a suit. You're a pencil pusher. You're nothing.' Everybody's different.

I do my own thing. I try every way to actually get [what I need]. I've had me bad days where I've chased it the wrong way and gone to gaol for it. I'm not proud of it but I give meself points for trying. My old man taught us that you're no better than the man in front of you and no less than the man behind you. But no-one [else] looks at you in that way and it sends you down and down. It sends you into a spiral.

All people want is bit of comfort in their life. It could be somebody to sit down and talk to for half an hour. Anything is better than nothing, but rich people don't see it like that. What's the difference between them having money and me having no money? Does it make me any less [of a person]? I met an ordinary guy the other day and asked him for a cigarette and we ended up chatting for four hours. That made me day. All people want is to get along with their lives and be happy, but how can you be happy if nobody wants to speak with ya? Everybody's got a story to tell and it's just a case of if somebody wants to listen to it. You learn off everybody. Every day's something new and once you have a smile on your face nobody can take that away from you.

It's like, if you don't have money to spend you're no good to talk to, so we won't bother talking to you. It really puts people down, and that's how people can't get out of the situation they're in. [It's like when you see] someone down, looking crook and leaning over [and] everyone just walks past him. They won't ask him, 'Are you alright? Do you want me to call an ambulance?' People won't do that. The only people who will stop are people who're in the same situation [as him].

The first time I ever slept outside I slept in a disabled toilet in a park because it had a lock. I was worried about somebody coming up to me and bashing me while I was asleep. At least I could sleep peacefully. I crept in there at one o'clock in the morning and had a couple of hours' sleep. As soon as I heard it was busy outside I got up and walked around with nothing to do. At first [on the street] I felt cold and alone and very disappointed in meself. You're sleeping on cement and the only thing keeping you warm are the clothes on your back. You feel miserable and hungry half the time. You [feel] you want to end your life, you're no good, just end it. That's what went through my head, and you just go around and find something [a reason] so you don't end your life. That's all you're looking forward to—the next day, nothing more and nothing less.

After a while you lose [the feeling of] wanting to be safe because you [almost] hope that somebody does kill you. But eventually you just realise safety isn't an issue no more. You're living out here on the streets, people don't give a fuck about you so why should they give a fuck about coming up and bashing you? You lose everything. You lose your self-respect. You lose your self-esteem. You lose your sense of pride. Once you lose your pride, mate, you've lost everything.

A lot of [homeless] people have trouble finding their pride. I've struggled just to keep a tiny bit of my pride still intact. It gets me by. But you've got to try harder to get to the next level. Then you get there and [there's] the next level after that. It takes time. I wouldn't wish these rich [buggers] to be in the life half the people here are in. It's not a life. We don't want to be rich; we just want to be comfortable [and have] a roof over our head.

Anyway, I got on track and then went off track. 'Off track' was sleeping in the street, and 'on track' was sleeping in a refuge. I had a short temper at that stage because I was shitty with meself and shitty with everybody because nobody wanted to help me out. Then I ended up helping meself. At least it was enough to know there was help if I could get it.

Yesterday I had no money to get a meal and this other homeless guy came up to me and gave me five bucks to get something to eat, no more said. He was in the same situation I was in and he gave me five bucks! I'll probably see him down the track and if I can help him then I will. If I see him picking up a couple of dumpies [cigarette butts] off the street I'll give him a couple of smokes. That's how the homeless community communicates with one another, but other people won't give you the time of day. They think if they give you money then you'll automatically go out and buy drugs. We might be in the 'lowlife' area but it doesn't mean you're a 'lowlife'. We're just the same as you people. How do they know I'm not intelligent?

I've walked past women and as I'm getting towards them they [grab] their handbag. I shake my head when they go past. There's only a couple of people [that do it], but why? I'm no different from you. If I had money they'd be looking at me different. We all bleed the same. We all die the same. Why can't you treat us the same? Is it because I'm a bit dirtier than you?

City life is a lot different from life outside of it. People outside the city know what it's like [to struggle]; they'll give you a chance. Here [in the city], if they're buying their kids' clothes, they'll say, 'Oh, kids, here's $300 to buy some sport shoes.' How can you spend $300 on a pair of shoes, mate? These people, when it's broke they throw it away and get a new one! My singlet is stained but it covers me. I wash it every day. Just because it's got a stain doesn't mean it's filthy. I shower, I clean, I keep maintained. I've got a healthy life.

People think if someone is on the street they can't get off it. But just because we're on the street it doesn't mean we don't want to get off it. I don't choose to be here. People think if you're living on the street you've got diseases, [they treat you as if] you're an infectious disease. [They think that if] they shake your hand [then] they're going to be homeless tomorrow.

When I was first on the streets I got very depressed. I just sat there and didn't want to talk to no-one. The first time at a refuge I was [age] seventeen. Then I went back to me dad's for six months and he treated me like a little kid. He wanted me to get a job and get sorted. It ended up where I was getting battered, so I moved away again. I got some money and got behind with me rent and got booted out. So I moved back and forth between here [Sydney] and Queensland.

Finally, they [employers] wouldn't give me a chance even though I had good references. It just puts you back in this situation. You just think that nobody wants to give you a chance so what's the point in going out and doing it? So you get bloody shitty at everybody. If I get a chance I think to meself, I'm not gonna stuff this up! But they don't give you one [a chance]. Everybody puts you down. Next minute you start believing it and [then] you can't get out of it. You're down and out [and] you think [to yourself] that you can't get any lower so you might as well dig the hole and wait to go in it.

If you live in a refuge and go out looking for a job people think, well, what are you doing living in a refuge? Shouldn't you be looking for a house first? [But] a house doesn't come without money and money doesn't come without a job. [The] priorities get mixed up. Priorities are different to different people, because if you've got money you don't worry about money whereas we have to worry about money to survive. Finding $10 to a person in my situation is gold. A rich person doesn't worry about $10.

I'm just barely surviving. I get just under $400 a fortnight on the dole and living in Sydney that [money] ain't [worth] nothing. The cheapest rent I can get around here is $150 a week. After that's gone, what do you have left to go looking for work and get food and clothes? So I save money by going to a refuge. You make do with what you can.

[What would help us] is free accommodation. You cannot go hungry in the city, but one thing you cannot get is a bed easily. Refuges are charging you to stay in a bed and if you haven't got money, you can't sleep. Mate, if you lowered the prices of the beds and stopped worrying about the money in your pocket a lot of people would be getting off the streets. If I had money and I could do it, I'd build a place. [I'd build a] big building [where] you go and sleep. In these refuges, you can't sleep during the day, so too bad if you [get] a job at night. Some people will get a night job, but have nowhere to sleep during the day!

In a couple of years [I'd like to have] a nice house near a beach. Somewhere I can relax and don't have to worry about being back in this situation, [with] a nice bed and a job. Ask for something you might have a chance of getting and you might get it.

John McDonald
age 41

I was born in Sydney in not unusual circumstances: two brothers, a sister, Mum and Dad. They're still together. I went to a private school and grew up in a nice area. Somehow, seven or eight years ago I fell through the cracks. I was disillusioned with life and just generally had a falling out in the industry I was in; I was working on feature films.

I finished film school in 1980 and did my first feature [film] in 1983, called *Robbery*. It was garbage; most of the things I worked on were. Except one thing I worked on in Alice Springs that had Linda Evans, Jack Thompson and Jason Robards in it. It wasn't bad. [I remember] Robards was an ex-alcoholic, a hard 1950s American man. [He was] almost a Jackson Pollack sort of person, transposed in a film set in the middle of Australia, out near Ayers Rock. I'm sure for him it was strange. [For me] working with someone like that was brilliant.

I did four or five features with the group I worked with. I did one [film] in Fiji and one in Vanuatu. I worked on the overseas freight, in charge of everything that moved. If you're held up even for a morning it costs a shit-load of money, so you learn responsibility. I've been there done that. [An ex-colleague from that group] Grant Hill has since done *The Thin Red Line* and *Titanic*. He was the Line Producer and got an Oscar [award] for that.

I got up to being a Second Assistant Director [but] that all fell by the wayside. I'd been blackballed in the business. The film industry is a very small world. Relationships became a bit irritating for me so I thought I'd have time out from those [too]. It sort of left more time for recreational drug indulgences. I tried heroin and coke [cocaine] a few times. Then, about ten or eleven years ago, it started being a bit more often. From [taking drugs] once every six months it [turned into taking them] almost every weekend and built up from there.

It didn't get to the stage [where] 'anything goes', because I never had to steal, shoplift, mug people or do robberies. There's no excuse to do any crime. I've had horrible habits, even a $500 and $600 habit each day but I never stole for it. [I've] never done any of that sort of stuff but I've sold drugs to support a habit. And that I don't feel good about. On the other hand, I only sold to people who [already] used [drugs]. I remember knocking back these kids because they were about eighteen and they were new on the street. They weren't happy [that I wouldn't sell to them] but I don't sell to children. If other people, straight people [non-drug using people] want to frown on that [they should understand] there wouldn't be a person that I sold to that I forced [into it]. A lot of us just did it to support our own habit. You don't become hardened to crime, you actually become more acutely aware of it and have more respect for its victims.

Occasionally, you'd find a wallet or a mobile phone [and] think, okay I'll return the wallet but the cash won't be with it. On the street it's considered reward money. Things like that [lost property] are a bit borderline. When you're on the street [the law] becomes a bit flexible. You have all these sorts of experiences and when you next find yourself homeless it [life] seems to become easier; it doesn't get any harder. Heroin makes it more bearable.

About eight years ago I got into selling drugs, supporting a habit. [I was] really becoming part of the Cross [Kings Cross]—not with the big dealers, just the street level of the Cross. You lose contact with the old friends you grew up with and end up with these new acquaintances, but they're your mates at the time. Being friendly with 'working girls' and the assorted riff-raff on the streets just became the norm. I didn't frown on anybody just because they did any [particular] thing, because they were people, too. We don't suddenly become 'different' [simply because we're homeless].

Even though [big dealers] still prey within our group there's still, believe it or not, a level of support. I wouldn't say [there's] a shoulder to cry on, but there's always an ear to listen. At the most unlikely of times somebody would shout you a shot [of heroin] out of the blue. It's just that you're related: something good has happened to them and you're totally in the shit. You're [at the stage] where you're thinking things couldn't get worse. I might as well laugh about it. Sometimes it can be just somebody giving you a cigarette or two and saying, 'Look, I've only got four or five left but here's half of them.' That can change your day. It may sound petty to other people but it's something.

The final slide for me happened when I was in a boarding house at Surry Hills. I suppose through using too much [heroin]. Although my rent was paid up [I had] a falling out with the manager of the place. I ended up losing all my possessions, all my clothing, everything. I came back four days later, after I'd organised somewhere to store my belongings, and I saw the remnants of it out on the street. As my mate [living there] said, 'John, you had really nice stuff.' He said [the manager] had put it out at nine o'clock that morning. This was about two o'clock [in the afternoon] and there was a handful of things left. [My friend] said, 'Mate, I even took a few things myself, I feel really guilty.' I said, 'No, forget about it.' It was almost like a cleansing. It's like you're straight back through the cracks because you don't have all those things that you'd need a place for. So when you don't need a place, you've got a reason to put a smile on your face and not to have a place. It makes it a lot easier to be homeless again. It becomes much easier each time.

I've been back under a roof a number of times but I keep sliding out, and now until I get community housing I won't bother. I've been on those [Department of Housing] lists forever. Hopefully it won't be long [until I get a place].

[The point where I felt I'd reached the bottom was] sleeping in the breezeway at the Paddington Town Hall. I'd be sitting in the morning having a cigarette and I'd see friends from my previous life driving to work in their nice cars. They most likely didn't notice me but I'd notice them. You look back on your life, realise where you are [now] and then it rams home what has become of you. It doesn't make you upset; it makes you introspective. You just go, 'Yeah, it's really nobody else's fault but mine.' Then you think, it's not so bad where I am. That's where the conditioning comes into it: you've adapted. Even though you are right at the bottom, almost underneath the grate of the drain, actually in the drain, [you think] that's an okay place to be. You think there are worse places [you could] be. The people I hang out with, the drop-in centres I go to, the food I'm eating—it's not that bad.

[Being homeless] you have less contact with friends and family. It's not when you are actually with them, it's after you've been with them for a few hours and then you go away. I always find that about half an hour after I've left them I become quite upset. [It's] because I think that I'm letting them down. It's not so much what they are thinking of me but what [effect] my actions are having on their lives and how they feel about their connection [to me]. They are the times when you think, I've got to do something, this [situation] has to change. So I go on the methadone program and try to get it together and end up in a place and get a little bit of work.

You try and do it [go on the methadone program], but for some reason something always happens. Sometimes [it] can be really trivial things, but you end up sliding again. [You might do] something nice, like lend somebody $300 to help them out. You think they're on their way back up [and you're] trying to do something decent for somebody, and then you get totally screwed for it. These things happen a few times and unfortunately your first reaction is [that] you've got to tighten your belt, [especially] when it's your savings and you're not getting the money back; it's upsetting. It's that trust thing when you thought you had a friend. Or maybe somebody steals something from you and then you'll find the only answer to relieve the pain [is to] just go and score [heroin]. Then you have a shot and it is enjoyable and you run into somebody and just indulge. It's easy just to fall back into it [a drug habit]. It's not complicated really, it's quite straightforward.

I've never ever stayed at one of the overnight places [shelters] where they've given you a bed for the night. It's either paying rent in a boarding house or a small apartment, or I've been on the streets. Also, without putting the shelters down, you'll either get thieved or there'll be a snorer and it won't make it enjoyable. It's nothing personal, because I've never really stayed in a place like that before.

Outside the library [in Paddington] there were three of us, [me and] two old guys, who'd been sleeping rough on and off for years. I learned how to fold cardboard boxes into a good little shelter. That was one good thing [I learned from] Italian John, an accordion player. You just get to know the size and fold of different cardboard that you just pick and go, 'Yep, there's my shelter for tonight!' Just from a pile of cardboard that's sitting flat against a wall! Now it's like a joke among the different people that know me and [have] seen where I sleep. [They say], 'John can build a shelter out of nothing. Just give him a handful of cardboard.' [I am] the architect! They're the fun times, because where we sleep there are rats and cockroaches by the thousands. Not that it stops them getting in. I always have food from a little cleaning job I do and I've found I need to have a little shelter to keep the animals and wildlife out of it.

There is trouble here and there [on the street]. It's mainly groups of young guys affected by alcohol and skylarking. They think it's really funny to grab your cardboard at three in the morning when you're asleep and root it out from underneath you. You go rolling, wake up and then they've taken off, laughing like hyenas, thinking it's hilarious. And you just think, you didn't need to do that, I was having a good sleep. Sometimes things come to that.

I was sleeping in a doorway at Central [Station] a couple of years ago and some guys did that [to me] one night. I pulled my boots on, ran off after them to Railway Square and as I approached them I thought I'd better slow down. There were a lot of people at this bus stop because it was four o'clock. There were eight of them. So instead of me walking to a definite bashing I just walked across the road and walked through Chinatown and thought, just chill out. I went for a walk and found a brand new pair of blue jeans with a really nice Timberland belt on them. They were all wet [but] it was only water, not alcohol or spewed-on or whatever.

There was no wallet in the jeans but there was forty dollars in cash. These guys did me a favour by ripping the cardboard from underneath me. I ended up better off because of something silly that they did. So you can turn it over and think, well, lucky they did that! That's the way I look at it. When something like that happens or somebody pinches your blankets—I'm onto my fourth set of blankets this year—I try not to get upset. I'll make a comment to a few of the guys where I sleep [and] say, 'Well obviously somebody needed them more than me.' And that's how I'm going to treat it. Why get upset? There's always a little bit of sunshine [to be found] on the flip side.

That view has helped me so far, but a lot of [homeless] guys have that [same view]. Some of the guys wake up in the morning and we've got a saying: 'Another day in paradise!' Obviously they're feeling good but quite sarcastic that morning and they come out with it. It's not like, 'Uh, another shithouse day.'

When the public are aware that you're homeless they normally don't know how to handle the situation. I've found that some people just like to throw money, they'll give you $20 or $50. You may have been chatting with somebody or you've found their purse and you've sat on the bench waiting for them to come back. Twenty minutes later they come back [and you tell them you found it]. You get talking and they say, 'That's really nice. I hope you didn't have an appointment to go to or I haven't disrupted your day.' I'll say, 'No, no I'm homeless. I didn't have anything better to do.' Straight away it changes the way they look at you, not always positively.

A lot of the time people's reaction is to give you a $20 note. Most likely, that day or a few days before, they've been [thinking] their life's not the way it should be. This or that isn't happening [to them]. They've had to pay for the car to be fixed. The plumber had to come. Then they meet a homeless person who's not whingeing and they think, here am I having a whinge. Their first reaction is to give that person money. I don't know if it's guilt; I don't know what it is. It doesn't even happen that often, but when it does it makes you think, why is this their reaction?

Most of the time you say, 'No, it's okay, I don't want your money. If you've got a few cigarettes you can spare that'd be nice.' But they go, 'No please. I don't care what you spend it on. [Hushed] You can spend it on drugs. Take it.'

You're like [apologetically], 'I don't want your money. I've enjoyed the conversation, I really have.' You're not fishing [for money]. The reaction you get from people when they find out you're homeless is to throw $20 at the problem or offer to buy you a meal. When you think about it, that kind of reaction is really quite nice. [It's better than,] 'Ugh! Look! Homeless!'

Most of the time the police are pretty good. Believe it or not, they keep an eye out for us. They don't like to admit it, but they do. Like, up at the State Library on any given night there'd be ten of us [sleeping] there. Around the other side there'd be another dozen of us. Now, the police know we're there but we've hardly ever had them come through. If they do they might do the occasional warrant check. There are cars broken into constantly along the Domain Road. We're never pegged for it because they know it's not us who do that. They know it's a different group of people: kids from a nearby neighbourhood. When the police know where you live and that you're a pretty straight bunch they keep an eye out and they don't harass us.

But if you're smoking weed [marijuana] endlessly, getting drunk, smashing bottles, shooting up and continuously involved in crime, well, [you will see] the other side. [The police] will then constantly come and see you, do bag searches, warrant checks [and then] apply the pressure. Like, I'm on methadone now. I still occasionally have a taste [of heroin], but all the guys know I go daily to get my medicine. I'm trying to do the right thing and I'm not breaking the law. So I'm welcome up there [at the Library]. I've been up there for coming up to a year and a half. They're mostly drinkers and pot smokers; there are all different groups. People might think they are all just druggies and drunks. [But] sorry, druggies and drunks don't mix, they hate each other. If you're on the road to recovery [and] you're trying to get better they'll give you a chance. You have to prove yourself constantly, but hey, that's okay by me, it keeps me on my toes. You become a good judge of character.

We're the people that are out at three o'clock or five o'clock in the morning. Maybe we can't sleep that night. There's nothing worse than lying on a piece of cardboard with a blanket over you, looking up at the stars and you can't sleep. I want to either go to sleep or do something, go for a walk. So you'll be out and you have to judge [somebody] by the way they walk or the way they're look- ing around. If [you encounter] a group of guys at four o'clock in the morning you have to pick what kind of situation it is. Because they might decide, 'Oh, here's a guy with a backpack. He's got his blanket, he's homeless, let's belt the fuck out of him.' You quickly learn to pick a [person's] character. You have to [constantly look out for it], because if they want to have a bit of fun, we're the ones they'll take it out on.

Don't get me wrong; that hardly happens. But when it does you want to be aware of it and avoid it. I've been robbed a few times at knifepoint but that was just [a case of being in] the wrong place at the wrong time. If two guys have got knives in their hands I'm not going to argue. I told them, 'Look guys, I'm homeless.' They didn't care. They said something like, 'Just give us your wallet, man. If we check your pockets and you've got more, we'll cut ya.' You don't argue with that.

That [particular] time we actually caught the guys through a few street people I knew that had mobile phones. The police picked them up two hours later. Unfortunately, it was my word against two under-age sixteen and seventeen-year-olds. They didn't have to be in a video line-up because of their rights. I was the victim; they got me for $980. That was my money to move into a flat and these guys had the remnants of it still on them.

We knew they'd gotten into a taxi, [which was found with] all four doors open and no driver [because] they'd robbed him, too. They located the taxi driver and then apprehended the two guys. But it couldn't be proven. They'd changed their jumpers so they looked slightly different; young experts. The detective told me they couldn't really charge these guys. I could have applied for Victims of Crime Compensation. I actually didn't do anything about the compensation because I don't believe in it. Like, if I was stupid enough to be where I was etcetera. It was just one of those things, wrong place and wrong time.

[The relationship with my family] is a lot better now. My father paid for my new teeth. I had terrible teeth to start with anyway, constantly breaking, but the heroin just accelerated it, and the methadone also. My father pays for my methadone. I now go and stay with my parents on the weekends. It's their way of keeping an eye on me. It's nice to see them happy about me for a change. I really look forward to seeing Mum and Dad and spending time with them. If they need any help with the gardening, or Mum wants the kitchen cleaned, I'm always happy to do it and they're happy to have me there. They still accept that I'm on the streets five nights a week, even though my father finds it hard to fathom.

There's a mate [of mine], Jimmy, who's moved indoors. He's been off the gear [heroin] for four or six months. I like to think that I've had a little bit to do with that, as an inspiration, because we talked about it. Now, he's actually overtaken me and I'm really just so happy for him. Every time I see him now I go, 'Jimmy, you look a million dollars', just to see his smile.

The [rehabilitation] programs can make a difference. I had it happen once, where I was just really down. In eight years of going to The Station [Drop-in Centre] I [only ever] used one of the services. I needed to speak with somebody, somebody normal, not one of my street friends. I ended up in tears, pouring all this stuff out, but I felt so much better after it. Just having that through the drop-in centres is incredible; it [can make] a world of difference. Just having somewhere to go where you know you can just sit down and nobody's going to say, 'Hey, don't sit there, man! Just get on your way!' [It helps] just knowing you've got somewhere that you can watch a bit of TV, make coffee and just be yourself [without] worrying about the next three or four hours. That's what makes a difference. Just to feel content.

They have to try new and different approaches [in tackling homelessness]. They can't just say, 'Okay, we provide meals, we provide x amount of beds each night.' They give funding to all the big charities; who knows where it goes. You just have to look at one of their monolithic headquarter skyscrapers [to see] they're in the business of charity, not in the charity business. I know if I want to go to them for help it's either their way or the highway.

You can't generalise [when helping people with counselling and support]. It has to be on an individual basis or even small-group basis. Even if you couldn't do it one-on-one, you could do it in groups of five or six. You [can] still try and tailor it to meet each individual's needs [instead of], 'This is what there is. These are the amount of beds we have. These are the amount of meals we can provide daily.'

There's the St Vincent de Paul van, which goes to Martin Place, [but] on two nights a month it just doesn't turn up. I don't know why. From what I've gathered they don't buy their food, they're given food and if they don't have food or volunteers they don't go out. When that happens I think there should be at least one person paid to come out [in a food van] for three or four hours. Here's this massive charity organisation [and] when it comes to grass-roots [work] and actual contact they're only volunteers. Nobody who's on a wage at St Vincent de Paul ever comes out in that van. I'm not whingeing, but it doesn't seem right. Some nights they [give you] dried bread rolls that are a couple of days old, that's the only food they have. They've actually turned up some nights [with] no coffee, no Milo, no tea, no milk—all they brought was the hot water. So they've got to go and buy a can of coffee. We're [left] thinking, God, where's the planning?

When they appeal for money to help the homeless, where does it go? I'm sure [current affair TV programs] would be aware of what is happening in charities. But if they did an exposé I would say there'd be a handful of corporate [charity donors] that would give money to advertise on their station, so the exposé would never be shown. [TV programs] skim the surface occasionally [but] it's too interwoven [with politics]. Some CEO of a company that donated $150,000 last year might be insulted, not like the story and pull their advertising from that station.

I can't see how the money is spent [by charities]. A couple of times we've taken the argument to a charity. Let's say they haven't had blankets for two weeks. You must have your name down on a list for a blanket and then they cross it off [when you get one]. Fair enough, it's a good way of keeping track. Let's say they get two hundred and fifty 'orders' for blankets and they might actually 'supply' eighty (some homeless people tend to move around and don't collect). Which list are they going to hand in? The 'orders' list or the 'supply' list? Whenever we ask questions we get a stock answer which has nothing to do with the question we asked. They think we don't have brains. Maybe they just think we're drug-affected, alcohol-affected or mental hospital rejects and that's why we're on the street.

At the moment I'm living at the Mitchell Library. My blanket and my cardboard are [stashed] behind two bits of timber that are leaning against a wall. We used to put [our stuff] in a garden area behind shrubbery but one day they decided to trim the garden. The only reason they decided to trim that day was because we were stashing our stuff there. We all lost our blankets and pillows. They knew very well it was ours. That was the Botanical Gardens Trust, which was so *nice* of them. So we don't stash it up there any more.

John McDonald

[These days] I wake up around six o'clock, roll my blankets, roll my cardboard and stash all that. Then I get down to McDonald's at Martin Place. I buy a coffee each morning for $1.50 [where] I can get a refill. I read their newspaper. Also, there are a lot of people that dump their [*Daily*] *Telegraph* or [*Sydney Morning*] *Herald* [in the street bins]. So I pick up a couple of papers and bring them to The Station [Drop-in Centre]—a bit of recycling! If people didn't have drop-in centres you'd lose the plot pretty quickly. I've banned myself from the Cross, Darlinghurst and East Sydney. I don't want to be even interested in who or what is happening up there. It'd be too easy to fall back [into my old way of life].

[As for the film career,] I think maybe I had my time. Without looking back, I just sort of look forward and see what happens. I know if I could work on one [film] I could possibly get my name back and get the roll-up again. I don't want to have that thing inside me going, you could have [done it]. So I'd rather be, 'Ah, you never know.' If it were a realistic goal [at the moment] I would go for it.

That's the thing [you learn] from being homeless and being on the street, the people you meet, the new views you form. I think I had a pretty good outlook [before], but being homeless has readjusted it. I've learnt a lot, which hopefully has made me a better person.

Ray Brown

age 33

I grew up with the saltwater people on the south coast of NSW, in a little town called Moruya. We grew up as fringe-dwellers, from the days of the Aboriginal Protection Act. We grew up [living a] nomadic life, moving from Wollongong to the Victorian border following seasonal work. We picked beans, peas, potatoes, fruit and veggies and stuff.

I go to Tranby [Aboriginal Cooperative College] now. The other day a guest speaker talked about how the 1980s were the best times for Australia. It makes me look back now and agree. It was easy to get a job. The lifestyle was fairly relaxed. I enjoyed it as a kid because you never had to worry where your next meal, your clothes or your blankets were coming from. That was your parents' responsibility, so all we [kids] saw was a good time, going to different towns, seeing different relatives [and] different ways of life up and down the coast. You can see such a variety when you're moving around, instead of staying in one spot.

That's what drove me into homelessness, that nomadic lifestyle. I left home at fourteen [as] this fresh-faced kid. I've never really laid my own foundations, because to me it had no relevance to stay in one place. I was too used to moving. I also went through drugs and alcohol and spiritual things. Then, a few years ago, I had my first child. He's nine now.

I went into different religions [such as] Buddhism and Catholicism. I'm starting to go back to the Aboriginal culture now. That [experience] made me more understanding and tolerable of society. The society we live in now is so hard, and you've got to survive and sustain yourself in it. I find [learning about my culture] is a release. It doesn't drive me backwards any more; it balances me. I'm not getting anywhere in a hurry but I'm not going down any more.

I came to Sydney when I was fourteen. I got my own place and had work and kept on going up and down the coast. That was my lifestyle from the 1980s to about 2000. I never worried about a feed or a bed because I knew I was always going to be provided for. In Aboriginal culture people always open their door. Greed and money were never in my culture and to me it still isn't. That was also a part of me that was confused.

In my culture if you see someone down and out, even a total stranger, you'll pick 'em up and help them out, no questions asked. Especially in big places like Sydney when you come from the bush. You start to mingle with a lot of people and I hung around with a lot of the elders. I felt more comfortable with them because they kept me on the right path.

Ray Brown

I roughed it and slept out in different places. As a teenager you're so resistant to cold weather and pressures, it's just like an adventure. I slept in old buildings and squats under bridges. I'd find little dead-end streets and parks. Before the grog and drugs I never really felt the cold or worried about the pressures.

I could have went home anytime I wanted to. I just left because I had an inquisitive mind and I just wanted to go out into the world. I still went home to Mum and Dad and that. I mean, the line was broken when I left at fourteen but I went back home when I needed to.

I look at it as a good experience. Now, at thirty-three, I'm start-ing to feel the cold weather and I'm a bit crook from all the drugs and alcohol I used. I've been doing that for nearly twenty years, so I thought I'd sort myself out before I started moving again. It's a new thing being in four walls; it's something different, but it's something I like. As an older person you need these things. As a young person you can be resilient and pretty much survive.

In 2000, I found out about my son and went looking for him to find out if he was mine or not. I had the paternity test; legal aid fixed that up. I knew that he was my son, but my ex-missus kept on telling me I wasn't the father. We're not in contact any more; she won't have a bar of me. The government took my son away from her; he's a ward of the State now. I only saw him once, when he was eight months old. That's pretty hard.

I've tried to be honest and upfront with DOCS [Department of Community Services]. I got told [by others] not to be like that with them but with my spirituality and my own learning progression I've got to be honest and truthful. That's what got ingrained in me early—that Anglo-Saxon society they keep records on ya. My track record isn't too good. I had to go to gaol on drug charges and got that out of the way in 1998.

I try not to worry about my son too much and the situation he's in. As a young person [trying to live with the system and society] I was affected because I didn't understand it, whereas now that I understand how it all rolls out the stress is gone and the depression comes and goes. DOCS have got their bureaucratic games they play, the same as every government agency, but I don't let it distract me now. I put my energy into something else, getting accommodation.

It took me ten years to see the truth and I'm aware of it now. I don't want to take all these hassles into my son's life; I've got to sort them out before. He's turning ten next year and I've got to get to him before he gets on the drugs and alcohol, that's what I'm working at now.

I've been staying at Mac Silva Centre [Aboriginal shelter] for six months now. At times, because it's only early days, feelings and emotions well up inside of me. It's part of the process of trying to stay still. But something held me here. On top of all that, society's lifestyle has sort of driven me to settle down and become independent for me and my son.

You know, the main reason why I'm at Mac Silva is it keeps me focused in reality [so I can see] how my life has been and how my life has got to change. I want to bring my son back out of that system [and] it's making me set my roots down. I don't have any animosity against anyone, my ex-missus or the system. I suppose I've come out the other end of it now.

Ray Brown

Looking back, I see it as like going surfing, catching a wave and going through a tube. It's all darkness around you in a big tunnel and you see the light at the end. I finally got spat out the other side, above the wave. My view is not a tunnel vision no more; I know I'm heading in the right direction.

I hope to get back to my own people. I want to move up north. I've put down for a [Housing Commission] house in Coffs Harbour. But my son's in Nowra, so I can't yet. For the last six months I know I'm home again because Sydney is the Aboriginal meeting place of Australia; a lot of Kooris come through. So I'm home again, but I'm not home. I get the real home feeling mixing with Aboriginal people. When I was homeless I was mixing around with Maltese, Portuguese, Chinese, Vietnamese, Lebanese. It's good to see the similarities, the good and the bad, because people are all the same.

The hardest part of being homeless was trying to understand who I was and where I fit in; what's my purpose? That was the main thing that stopped me. Being homeless never really worried me; I was young and travelling around different towns where there'd be street life and people to hang around with. I didn't have trouble. Most things I'd sussed out at a young age. That goes back to my spirituality; understanding myself and following the signals inside that let me know of danger, comfort zones; friends and enemies. You learn how to interpret body language. I had a pretty easy time. Even though I was naive, I was educated [at the same time].

I just survived. Drugs and alcohol really knock you down. You see people you've travelled with and all of a sudden you've found out that they've gone and it makes you realise that you're not invincible. I don't go to funerals any more. Death doesn't worry me because I know they've gone to a better place and that they're not suffering. I know everyone's time comes.

Things sort of smoothed out from 2000. It's been four years now; I haven't really gotten anywhere but I have got somewhere [at the same time]. I've made little steps. The main reason I want to get housing is because I want to build a foundation for me and my son. Like my parents said, 'Grow up.' You just seem to learn. Now they see that I'm progressing and it's making my parents' life a lot easier as well. I didn't realise I was carrying them down the path that I was going as well. I was such a stubborn, pig-headed young bloke with the Rock of Gibraltar on me back.

I grew up and I had a family and I didn't even want to believe I had a family. That was the way I felt [back then], that I was alone in the world. Now I see where I hurt my parents and me brothers and sisters. But I had to grow up and do that; I had to lose it to find it. That's the beauty I love about life. You wake up every morning not thinking that something bad is going to happen to you and then it does.

I've had cycles before of depression, stress, anxiety and anger. That has been going for the last twenty years. But I had to find my own way in life and the rewards are just starting to come to me now. I lost a lot of family and friends and I think that's what made being homeless even harder. That was from moving around and things you get caught up in. [Losing contact] is just the natural process [resulting from it]. It's starting to hit home and I'm able to think about it. Before it was like, I'm fifteen, I've got my whole life ahead of me. I'm comfortable now. Back then I was always looking and looking for a bed and thinking I had to be street-wise and smart. Some of the places where homelessness has taken me were unbelievable.

I understand it now. I don't fear it or try and make sense of it any more. It took me to some dark places, to some light places, to some strange places, to some scary places. I don't want to ever go back to living on the streets again. But if it happens, I'm not worried about that because I'll know how to look after myself, how to survive.

Networking is a good thing I found [dealing with] homelessness and just life itself. My parents grew up on the North Coast. My mother's from Gunnedah and my father's side is from Kempsey. We ended up down south because of the Aboriginal Protection Board and police trying to take the kids away. For me that was hard because I had to find a place to belong.

Living on the streets you pretty much make your own income and survive with your own instincts. Now, instead of sitting back and riding it out I've gained skills of communicating, understanding, relating and being in touch with society. It's been hard, but it's been a good struggle. I'm going to TAFE now and going back into my culture has opened more doors for me.

Going to TAFE, doing Aboriginal Studies, has given me more independence, more stability and reassurance [about] myself. I feel I'm going back now. I once grew up in Aboriginal culture and I knew about it, but only to a certain degree. Then, from my teens to now, I was in white society and culture. Now, it's like going back in a circle, I'm going back to my own culture. Everything I've learnt I want to feed back into it.

I'm looking from a life of youth, homelessness, addiction and mental health, whatever's beneficial to people. The only way to do it is to go through life and experience these things and understand that you've got to give back. I'm starting to want to give back. Things come to me and I can make more sense of it now. It's an invisible foundation and it makes [my life] more tangible for me. I'll never forget where I come from, what I did or where I'm going.

Tolerating life is a lot easier once you know where you belong. At thirty-three, it's a strange thing to try and understand where you fit in. [There is a] confusion about society. No-one tells you what your role is or where you've got to go and what you've got to do.

Coming to a place like the Mac Silva Centre brings it together and gives you a purpose and direction. Being homeless, you have no purpose or direction; you're just living for the moment. It's been a very long trot. When I look back and see all the people who passed away, because I'm a spiritual person, I wonder why I am here. I was given such a chance to get educated. Now I know I kind of wasted it, because [by all accounts] I should have been in that gutter with all my other mates, six feet under.

When I was homeless the public generally treated me like scum, a gutter-rat, lower than a dog's left nut. It kind of hurt. It made me angry at society, at the police and the system. It made me rebel more. You've got to go through this experience to understand it. I still see society in the same light, it's just that I'm not affected by it any more. But I feel for the people who are.

Ray Brown

I think that the people who've been through the mill [of home-lessness and struggle] have got to get the sorts of jobs that can benefit people on the street. It's no good putting someone in [the job] who goes to university or lives in a big house or goes around to Mummy and Daddy's or drives a BMW. Those people are not going to understand [homelessness]. They get into a position where they try to help homeless people but they don't understand them in the first place, through no fault of their own. I also believe you're [either] born with compassion [in your heart] or you're not born with compassion.

They need to encourage [homeless] people to get up there and not [let them] be put down or trodden or stamped into the ground to make them disappear. They've got to encourage these people to come up and grow and share their experiences with society, as well as the young people.

Liam

age 20

The names of people in this chapter are not their real names.

I grew up in Perth, and when I was about five I watched my mum and dad fight and then he left. So I didn't see him any more. My mum was a single mum for a while. She had a series of boyfriends who she most likely met at the church she went to. Later, I was told that the guy I thought was my dad wasn't my dad and that my real dad was a drunk, alcoholic, schizophrenic weirdo that probably lived out on the streets. Just before I was born she was coming off drugs. She said my biological father spiked her drinks and stuff for the few months she was living with him. I never got to meet my biological father, although I would like to meet him one day.

I was brought up with a church called 'The Potter's House'. It's changed now, but back then the church was very much like the Mormons. Apparently, I never cried as a baby because I had all

Liam

these different Mums looking after me; my mum never did look after me. She's in a different church now.

My mum was a sort of gung-ho charismatic Pentecostal-type Christian. When she was still single, when I was about seven, she made friends with this guy from the church. His name was Peter and he used to work near our house in a shop. After work he would come back [to our house] and I used to muck around with him because I was a cheeky little boy. Because he didn't have a bath [in his home] he used to have a bath at our place.

When I was about eight I used to peek in at him when he'd have a shower. One time he noticed me peeping on him and he was like, 'What are you staring at? Go away.' The next time I did it he was actually touching himself. As a kid I didn't understand what was going on.

One time he stayed the night. Mum slept in my bed and I slept in Mum's bed with Peter. Mum said it wouldn't be correct having a woman sleeping with a man in a bed. That night he abused me. At the time I didn't understand. It didn't occur to me to tell anyone or do anything about it. It wasn't difficult or anything. I just didn't know what to do. It only happened once, but he stopped coming over when Mum met Brendan and they had a de facto relationship for a year or two. Brendan had a daughter called Suzy who was five years younger than me. Anyway, Mum and Brendan eventually moved in together and got married after about two years. Then, when I was about thirteen they had my little brother, Mike.

Mum has always been very violent and very emotionally abusive. Looking back, I suppose I see that she just can't help the way she is. She's my mum and I still love her, but it's the things that she does. Growing up I can remember her doing horrible things with religion to get the devil out of me and making me spend hours writing scriptures from the Bible. She used to burn my books when I was really young because she would look through them and decide she didn't like the words in them. She would be physically violent as well. But I never once questioned her intentions. She's always meant good but she just didn't really understand [what she was doing].

When I was about ten I had a cold. There was an incident where we had a bowl of hot water with Vicks in it and I had the towel over my head. I was quite a stubborn child and I didn't want to do it [inhale the steam] because it stung my eyes. She shoved my head down towards it and I jumped back and the whole bowl emptied. I got second degree burns all over my legs. I was in hospital for about three or four weeks. Before that I was a good student but I think it influenced me stuffing up at school.

Even at that age I sort of realised I was different to other kids. I used to come home and be really upset and wonder why the other kids didn't like me because they used to pick on me a lot. Then I went to high school, which again changed things, because on my way to high school I used to go past Peter's shop. So I'd see him every so often.

When I started high school I was really concerned. I didn't know anyone who was gay. I didn't understand what it meant to be gay. I thought [being gay] was to be a big pansy or something. I didn't know any gay people and Mum didn't talk about it or anything. But I already knew that I was different and to be me was just that. Over the next few years I was very much the sort of person who would be what other people wanted me to be. I was always trying to be a few steps ahead of them to get the outcome that I wanted. I was like a mirror, reflecting what other people wanted. I would engineer situations to get what I wanted.

I was doing the same thing at home, too. When I was old enough to realise that I was gay I was worried that they'd find out. It was a panic in my head if they were to ever find out. But it wasn't just the gay stuff. I also didn't know how to interact. Like, when I was eleven and twelve I had this morbid fear of teenagers. I had friends in primary school but I was never allowed to watch TV or listen to music with them. I didn't want to be vulnerable, but I was really eager to be in the cool crowd, too.

At school it got to the point where I had to bash up people so that they'd think that I was cool. I was a nasty boy. I went to a private school and we even planted drugs on one of the school bullies so he'd get kicked out of the school. We got rid of a few of them.

Halfway through thirteen, Mum was talking to Peter and I got a job there [at his shop]. I worked on Thursday nights when it was busy. He used to give me extra money and used to drive me home. He used to say to me, 'Do you remember? Do you remember?' He'd do this weird thing with his thumb, mimicking what had happened [in bed with him]. I got really freaked. I talked in a very vague kind of way about it with my school counsellor because I used to see her every week in school. I thought I could manipulate Peter and use the situation to my advantage, to get money or what-ever. I didn't actually think I'd do sexual things with him. I didn't want sex; I wanted the money.

Liam

Around that time we went to this big horrible Christian church and I didn't want to go. I used to have panic attacks. They made me go to this youth group and I would try to hide or wait outside in the cold. On Sunday nights I used to dread it. Then, when I was about thirteen or fourteen I first tried to commit suicide, and I also tried to run away.

I always had to protect my stepsister, Suzy, from my mum because my mum got really jealous of her. Suzy wasn't home very often because she would also stay at her real mum's house. She couldn't see her dad very often. When she did come over he'd give his attention to her and my mum got jealous and would create this huge problem. There'd be arguments all the time, every second week. She'd tell Suzy, who was nine, that she was fat and ugly and no-one would ever want to marry her. Suzy and I used to go for walks in the park and we would talk about how we hated everyone and wanted to get away from it all, because my mum and Brendan were also arguing constantly.

I tried to run away because I decided I couldn't take it any more, all the pressure. I just thought, fuck it. I got up at three o'clock in the morning, packed my stuff, woke up my stepsister and said goodbye to her. She was really quite young at the time. That was really unfair of me to do that, I realise now. I rode my bike twenty kilometres to my grandmother's house but I had to go back the very next day.

After that I tried to commit suicide a couple of times with pills, a whole bunch of them. I grabbed whatever was in the cupboard and took them. I got really sick and threw up a lot. But I didn't tell my mum about it. Another time, and this was really horrible of me, Mum and Brendan were out so it was just me and Suzy. In front of her I stuck a knife into the power point. I didn't think it would kill me, I just thought it would put me in hospital.

What was going through my mind was [that] I seriously hated my mum. And every single day I used to dread Sunday. She just wouldn't let me think for myself. Like, I used to do art and she used to burn what I made. I just felt like I couldn't express myself or be myself. I felt like I was suffocating and she just wanted to break me. I couldn't take that and school was pretty full-on, too.

When I was about fourteen my mum found a job for me [at] a cafe. That was great, because at the time I was really rigid and thought I was a really nasty, cold, manipulative, horrible person. So I went to work there and I think it was really good for me. I made friends with one of the guys, Johnny. He was a very open, happy, bubbly person. I was still what I called 'the mirror boy', so I was reflecting that happy, bubbly character. He taught me how to be more myself and how to relax, that everything was okay. I worked there for about three years and got closer and closer to him. That got too much for me, I couldn't handle it. That was one of the reasons I left the job eventually.

Mum and Brendan were always separating and getting back together and always arguing. They'd hit each other with bottles and stuff. He was a big solid guy and most of the time she'd be hitting him, and she's quite small.

When I was about fifteen they had a really bad argument. He was going away for work and he said to Mum, 'When I come back, I want you gone.' This is right when I was having my first big mid-year exams in Year 11. So she went to stay at my grandmother's house because she was trying to find a place to rent. Meanwhile, I was staying between Peter's house and Cathy's, one of my mum's friends, for a few weeks.

One time, I was at Peter's house because I was upset about one of the fights between Mum and Brendan. Most of the time when I went to see Peter he was always trying to touch me. I knew what sex was because the more Mum and Brendan would say I couldn't do this and couldn't do that, I'd go and find out about it.

To them, everything was disgusting. I read about it at the library because I wasn't allowed to do anything else at the weekends. When I was at Peter's this time, I was on the computer and the Internet and he kept touching me and I just had no energy to resist him any more. We ended up in his room and that was when we started a relationship of sorts. I don't know exactly what I was thinking. I was young, stupid and I hadn't done that sort of stuff and he was the same age as my mum. He had a girlfriend during all that time.

So when my Year 11 mid-year exams were on there was all this fighting going on between Mum and Brendan, moving between houses, working and trying to study. I passed the exams, which is unbelievable. My mum eventually found a place to live and I moved in with her and my little brother, Mike. Most of the time when he was growing up it was me and Suzy looking after him; changing his nappies, feeding him. My stepfather worked six days a week and when he'd come home he'd cook my mum dinner. The only thing my mum did around the place was watch me and Suzy clean the house on Saturdays. She never did anything, except maybe sit on the phone. I really didn't like her back then.

Liam

When I moved in with my mum I wanted to play my stereo and Mum wouldn't let me. I said to her, 'If you're going to yell at me, I'm going to yell at you. If you're going to hit me, I'm going to hit you. I'm not going to take this any more.' That was after just a few weeks of being away from her! So she tried to stop me going to work and tried to make me late and stuff like that. We had these big huge fights and the police were called a couple of times.

I moved out into my uncle's house. He had a games room where I stayed. It was really great. I could come home when I wanted and spend my money on what I wanted. I couldn't stay at my uncle's house for too long, though. I was supposed to stay for two weeks but ended up staying two months.

At the start of Year 12 I moved into supported accommodation which had a few students, young people like myself. It was very transient, a lot of people moving in and out. I learned a lot there. I made some good friends and had to learn to live and interact normally. As I got older there was less personal editing and I was more myself.

After moving in [to supported accommodation] I went back home to pick up my cat. When I was growing up I always had a cat, and whenever I was upset I'd go out and pick it up and have a cuddle. Anyway, when I went to pick it up my mum wasn't home. Then I see my cat come out and it was walking funny. It had its leg caught in its collar and it was [jammed] into its fur. There was blood and pus [where it had dug in] and it was all grown over. I was horrified and so upset, it hadn't been looked after. To me, an animal is just like a baby. It can't say, 'Look after me.' I had to have the cat put down and I was so angry at my mum. I didn't talk to her for six months and I sent her cards back to her.

At school I was having big fights with my teachers because they knew I was bright enough to do well and I wasn't doing well. I was being really lazy. Then I met someone at school who was also gay and he introduced me to the gay scene in Perth. I still had this weird fear about going out in public. Early in the year we had the school ball and I was going to go to it but I was mortified, that sort of thing was a nightmare for me. I had some good friends and they insisted on dragging me along. I got Peter to buy me some really expensive clothes and I went to the school ball with a friend and I had a great time. Afterwards I thought, okay, I *can* do this!

It made me realise I could just go out and have fun. This was one of the reasons I kept away from the gay scene. So I finally went out into [the gay scene] with my friend for the first time. It was amazing to see two guys kissing! I enjoyed myself so much and I felt safe there. When I first went out I was a big slut. I slept with a lot of guys. I bought a new outfit every time I went out. I used to have a lot of spare money because I didn't pay much rent and I worked. I mean, I was still at high school and underage but still I could get in [to bars]. Some guys I'd be with would be rich. I would be what I thought they wanted me to be, like somebody more interesting. I wasn't being something I was not; I just emphasised some parts of myself more than others.

Some of the other stuff that I did I'm not proud of. Like, I went out with one of my friends to make her feel better about herself. She was feeling bad about her self-image. She found out about me [being gay] from another friend and that was that.

Liam

In Year 11 I'd found a book about bipolar disorder. Anyway, going into Year 12 I started becoming more manic and depressed on and off. I'd been depressed since I was about eight. Then, halfway through Year 12 I was diagnosed by one doctor as bipolar. I was still arguing with Mum, arguing at work, studying at school, everything was too full-on. I'm a very ambitious person, so I was really upset when I screwed up the [final] exams. I just couldn't deal with everything. That really upset me. I was working in restaurants and coming home [to the supported accommodation] at odd hours. I was essentially homeless and not eating properly. Then one night I went out clubbing with Peter. When we got home he tried to force me against my will [to have sex with him] and I said no. After that I told him I wasn't going to continue to see him.

So I quit my job and decided I wanted to move to Sydney. Perth just had too many memories for me. I told my mum I was moving. She decided to move [to Sydney] as well so she sold the house. She had found art stuff of mine in Perth, gay pornographic stuff, but she didn't confront me until we were in Sydney. I told her that I was gay and we had this huge fight. Then she decided to return to Perth and gave me an ultimatum to go back and live with her or stay in Sydney. So I said, 'No, that's it. I'd rather stay here than live anywhere with you.' She left and I was in Sydney with no money and no job—nothing. I just had my clothes. I didn't know anyone. I stayed at this horrible little place and after two weeks I heard about Twenty10 [Gay and Lesbian Youth Support Centre] and they got me into a share house.

In Perth I was pretty sheltered from drugs but when I moved into a share house my three housemates were all heavy pot smokers. I thought, oh my God, what are they doing with their lives?' I'd never done drugs or tried cigarettes even once. One morning I was sleeping on the couch and I woke up with some stranger licking me on the shoulder. I'm like, 'What are you doing?' He just said, 'You taste nice.' So I said, 'That's it! I'm moving out!'

I moved into a boarding house in Marrickville and that was full of odd people and mental people. I went back to Perth for a few weeks for Christmas and absolutely hated it. I was arguing again with my mum. Then I came back to Sydney and Twenty10 set me up in one of their flats which was great, although it was still temporary. I wouldn't have had the same [homeless] support system in Perth. In Sydney, though, it's really strange, because you find out about one place from finding out about another, it's like a chain.

I've been doing my art for the past two years now. When I came to Sydney I also started going to regular counselling again. I wasn't on any medication for my bipolar disorder. I thought I didn't need it. I thought whatever problems I had were mostly dealt with. I'd always blamed myself, because I thought that I had seduced Peter [when he'd abused me when I was younger]. My counsellor said that perhaps Peter shared responsibility, too.

In the end I decided to press charges against him. Since then the police have been investigating him. That's been really full-on. I had to tell a police officer where Peter had touched me. I was telling a big macho police officer all this and he wasn't even flinching. It was just so weird. So that's an ongoing process, obtaining enough evidence. There's compensation fees and blah, blah, blah. Also, the issue [with the case] is that when I was sixteen it was illegal for him to do that stuff, but now the law has changed and it's a legal grey area. They can still charge for the offences before then. When I told Mum about that stuff she felt it was her fault and that was the reason why I was gay.

Last year I started an art course and towards the end of the year I sold a few paintings. I got really motivated for the exhibition. I did a huge amount of work for it. I did sixteen pieces and sold five! But it was quite a dark year for me. I felt quite alone and I didn't really know anyone. I felt like a ghost. Then, at the beginning of this year I started to feel more grounded, a lot more stable. For me, feeling suicidal every few weeks is quite normal, but I haven't felt like that for quite a long time now. Despite what's happened to me, I feel it's made me stronger. I've become a lot more free.

Davo Marsh
age 47

Although I was born in Wagga Wagga, my parents moved before I was old enough to remember anything. My first memories are of Concord West, in Sydney. I remember the backyard and the backyard steps, just kid's memories. Then we moved again, this time to Adelaide, and after seven or eight years there it was back to Sydney again. My parents moved us around the city a lot, and I went to two different high schools at different points. After high school, at [age] nineteen I left home and went to live in temporary accommodation. I left home because I'd finished my [tertiary] studies. I'd failed my first year of a BA in Communications.

My mum had said that when I finished studying she'd cease to support me. That happened when I failed my first year. Mum had actually sent me to a therapist to find out why I wasn't studying. She didn't tell me anything about that being the reason she'd sent me there, though. That was all during my last year or so at home. The therapist never mentioned anything about study during those six months. So anyway, my therapist asked me to give up drugs.

My sister had some friends and they found me accommodation in Greenwich. I moved into a house full of [drug] addicted people, who I thought were really cruel. I only stayed for a few months; they asked me to leave without really telling me why. Well, the excuse was, 'We don't get on.' They smoked dope and hash and dropped acid. So I assume it was because of my promise to my therapist to give up drugs and that meant I didn't join in on any of their drug sessions. My drug use wasn't a big issue for me; it was more or less an adolescent thing.

After that I stayed with another friend of my sister. It was a house with just two of us. I was a very quiet person then, not like I am now. I didn't say much, and eventually he got tired of that and asked me to move on. I then moved into a rooming house in North Sydney. The usual one room with a shared kitchen and bathroom situation. I started to deteriorate from self-neglect, from the aftermath of the drugs and from having no friends. I was failing to attend to my personal cleanliness and had a room that was a mess. I got very sick, mentally sick. That was certainly when depression and psychosis was starting to set in.

I moved again after a couple of guys down the street asked me to move in [with them]. I got a girlfriend who was really a very nasty mole, to tell you the truth. So I decided to move back into the boarding house. I basically lay on the bed all day on my back with my arms and my legs spread out, just spacing out. I was forgetting to eat. Then Dad comes by because he is concerned about me and takes me to his place, a very small unit in Meadowbank. You see, because I was developing a mental illness at this point I neglected doing all sorts of stuff. I'd sleep in my sleeping bag on the lounge during the day. Dad started bashing me and I started having nervous breakdowns while that was going on. Eventually I ended up in a psych hospital.

Getting assistance for my mental illness basically landed in my lap. Dad finally, after all the bashings, took me to the community health centre and [I got] interviewed by a social worker and she said, 'How would you like a nice rest?' I said, 'Oh yeah, that'd be nice.' Then she said, 'Would you like to come to hospital?' I said, 'Hospital, hmm? You mean like, beds, wards, um … people on drips, stuff like that?'

At that time I was twenty-two. I'd never even heard of a psychiatric hospital. I said yes because I didn't have much will to say anything else. So I went to the psychiatric hospital. Basically I was grateful to be in a place where there was no violence; there was nothing else I could think of. I just sat in a corner on the ground with my back against the wall [and] my knees drawn up to me chin.

I soon got the idea of working on my mental problems with a therapist. I took my medication and that was okay. The diagnosis was that I was schizo-effective, which apparently is schizophrenia with some aspects of manic depression. It wasn't my diagnosis; at that stage I was just schizophrenic. Years down the track they finally decided schizo-effective, and I think it fits, so it's okay.

A classic thing happened when I first got inside the hospital. I was looking at all the people and there was this mural on the wall and

I'm thinking, I'm in a psychiatric hospital. They're all going to think I'm weird. Wait a minute, they're all weird, too! Okay, that'll be fine! Pretty soon a lady came along and she managed to liven up the place. She just had a gift of wonder at everything, a celebrational [wonder]. I mean, she definitely had stars in her eyes, but it was also down to earth, also practical. She had a balance. Everything [for her] was something to wonder at, and through the process of that she quite naturally created a real sense of life in the place, which was really nice.

After I left hospital, I moved into a commune down in the ACT. It was everything you think of in terms of a hippie commune, but there wasn't any free love or anything like that! I got kicked out of there, though. I guess it's just part of the stigma of mental illness. It just happens, and has done for times without number over the succeeding years.

[After that] I went into Canberra and wound up in a Woden Valley car park and saw this huge caravan. It was twice the size of a normal one. It had slogans all over it saying 'Jobless Action', 'Unemployed Workers Union' and stuff. So I popped in and asked for a cigarette and got one. Next thing I know, they're driving me back to their place and I got a bed on one of the lounges. I used to get up to eat or go to the toilet and feel free to observe what all these guys were doing. This is the early 1970s, so it was like the political underground in Canberra. They had Aboriginal activists there and 'save the whale' people, 'Friends of the Earth', all that stuff. I had a pretty happy time there, just relaxing and observing.

I moved again, from suburb to suburb in Canberra, [staying] in government accommodation. I just found myself vegetating in a room time and again. Some places would look wonderful but for me it had nothing to offer. I stayed in Ainsley Village, a housing co-op in Canberra. That site used to be an army barracks. When I got there [the rooms] were blocks and each block had a corridor down the middle with forty rooms on either side. They gradually pulled them down and built houses for people instead. That place was amazing. I don't why, but everybody in there was eccentric. Everybody was crazy.

I also went to a rehab. By this time I'd discovered a homeless drop-in centre in Manuka, a Canberra suburb. Then I got religion and saw my family and tried to convert them. I used to go of a night [to this drop-in centre] and one night I appeared pretty late. There were just two people there and I sat down opposite them and I felt like a spaceship taking off. Next thing you know I'm on the floor and my chair's flipped over; there was no visible sign of anything to tip it over.

Spontaneously, all my thoughts seem to be centred on Christ. I lay down there with all this new stuff in my head and eventually got up on me elbows and prayed the first real prayer of my life. 'Dear God, strength in me, strength in my mind, strength in my will that I may work in your garden.' And then I flopped back down on the floor again. They let me hang around for as long as I needed. They asked if I'd like a cup of coffee and I went home.

Ever since then, the bulk of my thinking has been centred around Christ. In the time leading up to me discovering that drop-in centre, they used to feed me plate after plate of chicken stew. I'd eat about half a dozen plates of chicken stew in one night. Anything is good when you're hungry, let me tell you that! It's amazing what it does to improve your taste buds. I'd drink cups and cups of coffee; that's how I came to have a coffee addiction. So anyway, I decided I wanted to see my family and convert them. I hadn't really been in contact with them during that time. I had visited, going back and forth between Sydney and Canberra, but this time I made up my mind to convert them.

When I got up there [to see them] I didn't even know half the stuff they were talking about. I just got to sit there quietly. I soon realised what I needed to do was sit back in the family and not make a primary aim of converting them. In the process of me just pursuing my beliefs a good number of them have converted. It wasn't through my efforts. I believed very much that it was God doing the work. I was just stepping out of the way and letting him do his work.

In the early 1980s I'd been running up credit beds in all the [Sydney] city [homeless] hostels: Matthew Talbot [men's shelter] and Swanton Lodge. Credit beds are where you could get a bed when you needed it and chalk it up on credit. If you got a bed on credit, you had to pay them for it [at a later stage]. There were several of us that lined up in front of the staff and were told that we'd get no more credit beds. If we wanted them we'd have to pay for them [upfront]. They were speaking on behalf of all the hostels we had run up credit at. And they said if we wanted to pay, we wouldn't get one until we paid back what we owed. Of course that was financially impossible for me. So I slept outside for the first time in my life.

I went to sleep in Hyde Park and woke up in a bed. There was sun shining through the window, birds in the air and blue sky. It didn't occur to me how I got there. I was just so grateful to be there. I get up and there's a Catholic study Bible on the desk and one other bed in the room. I go downstairs and there are Christian books and Bibles on the bookshelf. Then, that very night, the guy who ran the place, it was called St Francis Community, came in and they had a charismatic prayer meeting. The church I'd gone to in Canberra was also a charismatic church so I felt right at home.

I've got no memory between falling asleep in Hyde Park and waking up in a bed in a house. I didn't wake up at all [during it]. I just attribute it to God in His grace. Well, they do say that God moves in mysterious ways. Anyway, I wasn't there for a long time. They had a small cluster of houses around Surry Hills and I sort of moved from one [part of church housing] to the other. I went to another place in Chalmers Street. During the next twenty years that was my main base. It [the shelter] was run by Sister Pauline Fitzwalter, a Good Samaritan sister in the St Francis community.

[Eventually] that place had to close down because of trouble. A Lebanese gang were chucking dead ducks over the back fence. It was obviously a hint: 'You guys are dead ducks. We're gonna get you.' Apparently they broke in through the back door, which was pretty fragile. They then pack-raped a girl who was living there. So anyway, the house closed down soon after that.

After this period I spent two years in a place called De Porres House, which consisted of three terrace houses on Bourke Street, in Darlinghurst. The middle house was a drop-in centre during the day and the houses either side were all residences. It was the only time that I had a room on my own. I had my stereo and was building up my Bob Dylan collection.

It was basic rent, and the best thing about it was there was wall-to-wall people whenever you wanted them. When there wasn't wall-to-wall people, there was my stereo. [It had a] turntable, a double cassette and CD through the auxiliary channel! Eventually I had to leave there. Somebody played a dirty trick [on me]. [One guy] set me up [so that] I got kicked out so that he could get a room; at least this is my theory.

I went back to [the St Francis Community] and stayed there for a while but the longing and desire to be back in the city was very strong. Eventually I let myself get caught smoking [cigarettes] in my bedroom so that they'd kick me out and send me down to Matthew Talbot [Hostel] in Woolloomooloo.

By that time, all my bed credits had been forgotten and I knew how to make my commitments [to pay up on time]. It turns out they changed it to be a maximum of three months to stay. They phoned Edward Eager Lodge [homeless shelter] and I went there, and they also had this three-month limit. They made a special exception in my case; for some reason that I don't understand; they regarded me as chronically homeless.

Whatever the reason, they decided to stretch the limit for me and keep me on until they found me a place. That led me directly to where I am now, [in semi-independent accommodation] in Darlinghurst. I've got my canvas [artwork] in the style of a stained-glass window, a bookshelf, pictures of the Holy Spirit and my paintings on the wall, my multicoloured rug and my little stereo with the turntable.

Davo Marsh

The specific aim of this place is to find you permanent accommodation; they have a two-year program. It's the best place I've had and I've been here for the best part of two years. I've got two months left. If they haven't found you permanent housing by then, they will stretch it to a point where you can stay longer.

[During my stays in shelters] such as Matthew Talbot and the old Swanton Lodge [I also stayed] in Proclaimed Places.[4] They soon made it so that you had to be intoxicated [to get a bed]. There was this scam where if you wanted a bed for the night you had to find a bottle of alcohol and put it on your breath and go [while breathing forcefully at them], 'I want a place for the night!' But the staff have long since sussed that one [out]!

My family contact, during all this, had turned into an ordinary type of relationship, so that's cool. At one point when Dad kicked me out I had no money at all. I had no ID [so] I couldn't get the dole and that was how come I had problems with the credit beds— I just didn't have [any] money.

I embraced that life [of homelessness]. It was painful and joyful at the same time, cruising along the road in Kings Cross, watching all the buskers, observing the passers-by and stuff like that. [You could] strike up an instant friendship with someone. It was partly the inspiration for my poetry.

The main influence [of my poetry] was what I picked up in the community, spiritual understandings, spiritual ways of dealing with the problems of homelessness. That's what my book *A Street Spirituality* was all about. Giving ordinary people [in the public] a perspective on homelessness. Also, from my point of view as the writer, [I wanted to give them] spiritual methods to deal with street problems, speaking to street people so that they could learn to lead their lives better.

My experience [of the public] when I was homeless was [one of people] not acknowledging each other. Sometimes in church I thought, why the fuck aren't these people interested in me? You know, sort of wanting, but being unable to promote a mixing between the two [groups]. It wasn't a judgement [by them, of me]; it was pretty much an 'unawareness'. Pretty much, you aren't seen. People don't even realise that they're not noticing you or the feelings you have. I think it's to do with personal presence. When you're homeless you have no rights, you're moving among crowds and [it's like] you're being anonymous among them. Then, when you come into that church situation [it's like] you're still anonymous.

But to help the homeless [practically] there certainly needs to be another structure to house people, even if it is on a three-month basis. They could have built one across the road from Edward Eager Lodge. That would definitely help. The charities are doing the main part. All the hostels, it seems to me, are run by charities. There's Foster House [run by The Salvation Army], Edward Eager Lodge [run by Wesley Mission] and Matthew Talbot Hostel [run by St Vincent de Paul].

One thing that government does need to do is provide funding. These places wouldn't exist without money from the government. For instance, Missionbeat goes around and picks people up off the street and takes them to a shelter or a hospital or whatever they need. They don't operate after eleven at night and the reason for that—I got this from my brother, who used to drive for Missionbeat—was that there were 'not enough people helped for dollars spent'.

That's when people are in most need. Money is necessary, but to think that it's [homelessness is] all a matter of money, which [is what] the government seems to think, is a gross misconception. It's supposed to be about people's welfare.

Swanton Lodge shut down a little while ago and [the] Matthew Talbot [Hostel] was forced by the government, under threats of withdrawing funding, to have one section for rehabilitation. That immediately cut the beds by a third. Foster House has been lucky to rebuild their place nearby to the old place.

The Minister at Edward Eager spends a grossly disproportionate amount of time on paperwork. Her job isn't as an administrator, to shuffle papers on a desk; her job is to provide spiritual support for the residents. You never get to see her downstairs with the people. She does a church service on a Sunday and Bible study on a Wednesday evening and that's about it. The rest of her time is spent with paperwork. She's retiring soon. There will be another minister in her place and an administrator freeing them up to do what he or she is meant to do.

As for my plans, hopefully I'll get permanent housing around Darlinghurst or nearby a support network. I've written one poetry book and self-published over one thousand copies of it. Hopefully, I'll have a second book [over the next couple of years]. In the end, the best explanation and description I could give of homelessness, from my view, is to let my poems speak for themselves.

Nathan

age 23

I come from the NSW South Coast, from a fairly well-off family. About two years ago I left home. At the time I was told to get out, to get out [in the world] for myself. [My parents] were happy for me to go and do my own thing so I thought I'd go up to Gosford by myself. At the time it was hard for me because I had gambling problems. That started when I was about sixteen [years old]. One of my mates showed me how to do it, the horses, and I just watched. I thought, shit, I can do that! It was pretty good, I got about $120 from it.

After that, every week I spent my pay on the horses. I had a job at Woolies [Woolworth's]. It [finally] got to the point where I [got] credit cards [to pay for gambling]. I just got into so much trouble. [My folks] got sick of helping me out. They wanted me to move on.

Nathan

When I got up to Gosford I had to sleep outside the tourist information centre there. That was my first time [out on the street] and you had people walking past all the time looking at you. People would walk past at four o'clock in the morning making so much noise, or they'd steal your gear when you were asleep. So I didn't sleep well; I'd always wake up tired.

The most terrible experience I had was when I was sleeping up in Gosford. I was asleep and this rat came right up close to my face and started sniffing me. I opened my eyes and just saw him there and looked him in the eye.

I stayed up there for about three months [until] I went to stay at Vinnies [St Vincent de Paul]. From there I went onto Woy Woy and ended up sleeping at the back of the shopping centre. There were cockroaches and rats; it was shithouse, man. The cockroaches [would] climb through my hair. I stayed there for about three months and came straight to Sydney about a year and a half ago.

At the time I was living off dole cheques. My folks knew, but they wouldn't help me out. [It was like] once you're [out], that's it. When I first got into trouble gambling I rang up Gamblers Anonymous. They couldn't help me out. All they said was, 'It's your problem. What do you want to do?' I said I wanted to find out why I was doing it; what makes me go back to doing it again. They tried giving me solutions like giving my parents my money. I kept going back, straight from the dole queue to the TAB [betting shop], and wasting it.

When I first came down [to Sydney] I stayed up near the State Library with all the other fellas. It's like a convention up there! I just set up under a ledge-like thing for a roof and put up some crates to keep protected from the wind. The elements aren't too bad. The cockroaches are, though, when they climb over you when you sleep. It's not too bad up there; you get a bit of food every Wednesday from St Paul's Mission.

Although I'm still gambling, I'm trying to cut it down so I can try and settle down somewhere and get a job. Within the next six months I want to get settled somewhere. Hopefully I'll find a place of my own [and] I wouldn't mind getting into acting—I've got this experience [to rely on]!

It has woken me up. [For example], most homeless people you speak to are very, very nice people. When I was living [back] at home I just thought all homeless [people] were psychos. They're just people and they've just got their own different problems. Most of the people [I've met on the streets] have been living there most of their lives.

A couple of them up at the [State] Library tell me I have got to [get off the street]. I want to get out of it 'cause it's not really a nice thing. I haven't had any troubles, 'cause I've been staying in with a good bunch of guys [at the State Library].

The hardest part of being on the streets is probably just the mental side because I'm living [there] and I've got a problem [with gambling]. What am I going to do about fixing it? What if something goes wrong? I've got nothing to fall back on. I mean, I can go to The Salvation Army for free but it makes it easier for me [to spend my money]. It's a cycle now and I'm trying to break it, but my heart's hurt. It gets you really down on yourself. Even though you know inside you shouldn't be doing it [gambling] you just can't help it. You just want to win a bit more.

Nathan

My parents just want me to succeed at something, to see me happy, married, having a good life [with] a good job. It's difficult for them and for me. I'm in contact with my family as much as I can be, just to tell them I'm alright.

Linz
age 36

I came to Australia at the end of 2001 from Auckland, New Zealand. I went to Melbourne, where I lived on the streets and did a bit of work, and I've [also] travelled around Australia. I've been [homeless] for about eight years on and off. [Originally] I started living on the streets because I didn't want to [live] within the establishment; I wanted to do my own thing.

I come from a good family. [They] don't know what I'm doing [or] that I'm homeless. They think I'm living with mates. The last thing I want is for them to be worrying about me and I'm old enough to look after myself. If I want to get off the streets, I'll get off them. But I don't want to [yet]. It's my freedom and it's given me time to think about my future [and decide] what I want to be. I didn't want to rush into doing this and doing that. It awakens my horizons when I'm on the street. That's what I set out to do.

Linz

When I first set out on my own I didn't know I'd end up living on the streets. How it first started was I bumped into a couple of friends back in Auckland and they were on the street. I had a job, the normal working life, and every time I walked past them on the street I'd say hello. Then one night I went to a tavern, had a few beers and walked out and they were having a few drinks and I just ended up joining them and I slept on the street where they slept.

I woke up the next morning and went, 'Far out, I had a good night.' I think that's how I started enjoying the streets. I guess I wanted to experience what they were doing and so I tried it myself. I took it from there. I started getting into trouble, breaking and entering shops, getting caught and then getting sent home to my parents. That was all when I was about twenty-eight. I really just wanted to experience life. To try and get into a better lifestyle than my old lifestyle, where I was working and not saving. I was blowing my money at the pub and gambling. That was the life I wanted to leave behind.

When you're living in a stable establishment there are certain boundaries where you [have to] do this [and] do that. When you're living on the street you don't care what you do. You can go up one day and down the next. Living in a house it stays [emotionally] on one level. So in a way, I like the street. What I find is that you experience the life that you see. You still catch up on the news—you pick a paper out of the bin and read what's going on in the world.

I'm starting to get sick of it, you know. You see cases of homeless people that have really bottomed out. You say to yourself, that guy's had a bit too much [of the homeless way of living] because he doesn't care what he wants to do. So you say to yourself that you don't want to get that far [or go] to that extreme. There's a side of me that still has sanity. I still take pride in myself even though I'm walking the streets.

There's a part of me that has got pride to say, 'Who cares if I am on the street? I'm doing what I want to do.' [But] I still don't want society to look down on me and think, you're just a bum and you've got nothing. Well, I feel you're just the same as me. If we changed sides I don't think you'd survive. If you started from scratch and had nothing and I chucked you out on the street, you wouldn't be able to handle it. [Then again] if I changed sides to go into an office, I wouldn't know what to do either.

[Through] being homeless I've learned to respect myself, respect other people and respect the street. I'm always humble towards people that are more fucked up than I am. I don't judge them; I just look at them and I wish I could help. I have problems of my own and helping this person [or that person] would be another problem [for me]. The world is a pretty sad struggle. It won't be a perfect world until people wake up to themselves and realise they need to treat every other person in the world as a human being.

People should [also] look at children; they're our future [yet] children are the ones that suffer [the most]. We continue to send innocent people to war and the last thing their children should [have to] ask is, 'Where's my dad?' With the war over in Iraq it is the innocent people who die for nothing. People and children there [in Iraq] have got it hard. They don't even get to live their life and here's me, a 36-year-old on the street, but I'm lucky to be alive.

Linz

The hard side of being homeless is trying to fit into society where people look at you as if you're strange. I wouldn't walk down the street all ratty-tatty and torn, [but] who cares if someone has a hole in their shirt? You just don't look down on them; they're people as well. I'd rather a person smile at me than look at me in disgrace. When someone just walks past you and looks at you as if you're the dirtiest piece of shit, that triggers negativity. But I don't let it get me down. I just keep it to myself.

I've slept in [parking] garages, an abandoned house for two months, public toilets. Sleeping in public toilets was the lowest I've been but it was only because it was a rainy, windy night and because sleeping in a bus shelter you'd be bloody freezing in the wind. When you sleep in a public toilet you try to hold your breath the whole night!

One time, for a couple of nights, I slept in a stolen car [that was] left on the side of the road. When you see the yellow sticker [tow-away notice] you figure you might as well be part of the furniture with the car. During the summer I've also slept on beaches under the stars. But in cold weather you've got to have a roof over your head. At the moment I'm staying [outside] the NSW State Library. There's a few us that have our quarters up there.

When I arrived in Melbourne from New Zealand it was coming to the end of summer. I had to walk around the streets to get myself tired so I could go to sleep. While I was walking I [would] look around to see if I could find a bed and I found a [public] park. I had no blankets, just a sleeping bag, and I found a bit of [ground] protection like an under-blanket. Then I found a place to stash my stuff. I [also] came across this work site and found a big bundle of that black plastic sheeting they use in laying foundations. So I made a little tent in the park right out of harm's way and public view. I like to have a bit of privacy.

I was there for about four and a half months [and] I never got caught [by the authorities]. There was a bit of paranoia in me, like, 'What was that noise in the bushes?' But I did sleep with a little pocketknife, which I really shouldn't have. The fact is there are strange people out there and you never know what could happen, so I only had it for my own protection. You could be sleeping and wake up with a knife in your belly. That's the sort of thing I don't want to think about but it could always happen. I've had a few things happen, nothing major, but I just back off and say, 'I don't want no trouble. I just want to do my thing and get out of here.' I haven't had any really bad experiences yet—knock on wood. I can handle myself and fend for myself.

In Melbourne, I got work doing labouring and car detailing. When I first started getting work I got off the street and stayed at a backpacker [hostel] for about three weeks. I couldn't handle living there so I found a little shack and started squatting there for two and a half months. I'd wake up every morning and just go to work. That's when I had problems with marijuana, alcohol and gambling; they took a bit out of my money. I was wasting it [money] and not looking forward to tomorrow. [That's when] I rang my parents and they wired a bit of money.

They got worried, and my mum was asking, 'What are you doing? Get your shit together.' She told me to save my money. A year down the track I haven't borrowed [any more] money. Like,

Linz

I'm old enough to look after myself and [I wanted] to shield her from [my situation]. For the first couple of months I was ringing her but now I only just ring her when I'm happy or when I'm sleeping in a nice double bed. The last time [I called] I told Mum I was on the streets but I only told her I was there for a week because I had nowhere to go. She couldn't sleep because she was worrying about me. I had to tell her a white lie the next time. If I said I was on the streets, she would say, 'No, no, no. I'll send you some money and you're coming home.'

I've got friends with houses and they took me in off the street but it doesn't last long—about a week [usually]. I minded a house for friends of mine in Melbourne for about two weeks and when they came back I just thought, there's something missing. They didn't want me to go, but there's a big world out there and I wanted to do my own thing.

On the street it's a big stage. I wouldn't have experienced some of things I have if I was in a house watching TV. You have to watch it in real life. I've seen live sex shows on the street, drunks, people shooting up, these are things I never would have thought about and here they are in front of my eyes. I just sit there and laugh sometimes, just thinking [in amazement]. I carry a diary with me every day and I write down what I've experienced. I write it just to hold onto as memoirs. Down the track, when I won't be here [on the street] I can just pop out the diary from that year and [read back on it].

Like, one time, me and a friend were camping in a city park. We were having a few smokes and out of the blue this 'working girl' comes around the corner dressed like a stripper, very revealing. I said to me mate, 'Man, are we that stoned or what?' He's going, 'No man, that's real! Where'd she come from?' She walked past us and said, 'Am I disturbing your sleep?' We said, 'Nah, nah, you're alright.' She just squatted right down in the corner in the light and pulled out this syringe. My mate said, 'Aw, she's going to shoot up.' I'd been on the streets for a while then but I'd never seen anyone shoot up. I've never done it in me life and I don't want to, so I said to her, 'Is it okay if I watch?' She said, 'Yeah.'

I watched this lady get down on her hands and knees right under the light. She pulled up her sleeve to try and find a vein but she couldn't find one. I said, 'Are you alright there?' She said, 'I think I've used every vein on my whole body!' I asked her how old she was. She said she was about forty or something. I asked her how long she'd been doing heroin and she told me [she'd been doing it] for about twenty or twenty-five years. Then she missed a vein and went into funny spasms. That was freaky. We got out of there.

Another time I was crashed out in a bush in Newcastle listening to my Walkman. In the corner of my eye I could see something and I turned around and looked and there was this figure coming through the bush. I had a proper look and [saw] it was a young woman, she was pulling up her dress to have a leak! I said, 'Whoa! Are you right there?' She looked up at me, pulled up her pants and she said, 'Fuck! Where the fuck did you come from?' I told her, 'Well, there's a women's toilets right down there.' [I pointed to where they were.] She ran out of the bush and went off to the toilets. I watched her go back to these two cars where there were all these youths and heard her say, 'There's a guy in the bush and he's sleeping there!' I could hear them all laughing about it and then they left.

I mean, she had to go and pick a place [to pee] right next to me! I had to say something. I didn't want to scare her or anything because she could have gone to the cops and told them there's a stalker or a rapist in the bush perving at a young woman having a piss! If I was a sick, fiendish mind I would have just sat there and watched it, but there's nothing great in watching somebody having a pee!

Over time I've struck up a few friendships with other homeless people. I took a liking to a guy I met. He seemed to have his head screwed on, a pretty intelligent person, and I asked him why he was on the street. He said he had a few things to sort out. The story was he got this girl pregnant and he didn't want to take on the responsibilities and that's why he hit the streets. We had a beer and started talking in the nights. One day he said he had to go back and face the girl [he'd gotten pregnant]. We were in a park and his mobile rang. It was his girlfriend; she had a miscarriage. He was happy and I asked him why. He said, 'She was a real bitch to me.' I told him, 'Well, that's your view.'

We parted and I didn't see him for months. Then [one night] at three o'clock in the morning I felt this tap on my shoulder and he was there. He had a slab of VB and a big envelope of sticky buds [of marijuana]. He was in town for the night and we sat there and had a few drinks. [Eventually] I said, 'I've got to sleep now.' He said he had to go and for us to keep in touch. We'd had a good experience together; I could talk to someone who sort of had their head screwed on.

Linz

Some guys [on the street] when you try and talk to them they're in a world of their own. Like, some guy would [point to buildings in the city] and go, 'I named that building and that one.' I knew this one guy and he'd tell me that he'd named the McDonald's [restaurants], Burger King and designed the Sydney Hospital. I told him, 'Mate, those buildings [Sydney Hospital] were built in the nineteenth century. So how old are you, man?'

I look at the ex-mental patients, and think they really need help. They don't know what they're doing. What pisses me off is the governments, the institutes or the mental hospitals, whoever is to blame for leaving them out there. They should be in there getting help. There's no support for them [living on the street].

I once saw this lady walk through Martin Place with no clothes on, except for a little backpack, in the middle of the day. She was in a world of her own. How could they leave her to walk around the street in the day, naked? I'm sure she would have known it but the brain wasn't there. People were just laughing at her.

I mean, [you could tell] she must have had a pretty fucked-up life to be walking through the middle of Sydney naked. She would have been [aged] in her early forties or so. If I'd had a blanket there I would have done the right thing. I wouldn't want to see my mum or my grandmother walking down the street like that.

I've come across one homeless guy who'd been a managing director [of a business], [earning] over $1500 a week. He'd blown his money and life on drugs, heroin. He said, 'Look at me. I used to have a good life.' I told him he could pick himself up again and that's what he was trying to do. I said, 'I lived a good lifestyle too, but I blew it. Now, I have to start again.'

Linz

When I get off the street it's going to be better than the last lifestyle I had [before I became homeless]. I don't want to do labouring for the rest of my life. I want to try and help people. [I'd like to be] something like a social worker or a probation officer, something that's in community health. It gives a good feeling in your heart, in your soul, to help someone who's more down and out than you [are]. And also I've had that experience, too. I just like helping people; that's all it is, really. A lot of people around these days don't want to help [others], they just pass the buck. There are people out there who think they're helping [others] but they're basically pawning you off, passing {the problem] further down the line.

My friends would just freak out if they knew I was living on the street. They'd go, 'Are you crazy or something, man? What do you do that for?' I don't want to drag them down into my hole; they've got their own lives to lead. Maybe [when it's over] I'll give them my diaries and just say, 'Read that, mate.' When I become a dad I'll tell my own kids to read it [and say], 'I don't want you doing that.'

There's a place where we all meet at the end of the day in Martin Place. A few of us 'streeties' will go to the food van where you sit down and have a feed and just watch people going by. People look at us like we're a sideshow, sitting in a line on our milk crates. I kind of get embarrassed because I'm in the line as well. I try and hold my head down. I shouldn't be like that. I should be proud of myself [in front] of people wearing Armani suits and that, but I can't handle the looks and stares. Thinking about that makes me angry [enough] to want to get off the streets.

Linz

If I was working I wouldn't turn a blind eye to people on the street because there's some decent people out there that are clued-up. They're only homeless because of addictions. In their past lives they had close family and friends.

I mean, I can be gullible, and you meet some guy who says, 'Come have a few beers.' Suddenly they could lead you to gaol. I'm here to keep my nose clean and I believe in karma. I believe in the 'Big Fella' and ask for help to get by from day to day, to just look after me. I might say [to Him], 'I've drunk all my VB, smoked all my bongs. I shouldn't have gambled again. But I'm trying to help myself.' But the Big Fella knows there are things I keep to myself as well, who I am inside.

If you walk up to Martin Place from four-thirty [in the afternoon] onwards, you'll see us up there. There's a supplier that brings food from some take-away that they'd normally chuck away at the end of the day. I'm against people that you see walking around the streets saying, 'I'm hungry. I need money for food.' Get yourself together, mate, you must be looking in the wrong places. Go to food vans or drop-in centres. I don't go hungry. That's what I like about Sydney [if you're homeless].

And there are people who give us bags of food. There's much appreciation [among the homeless] for people to do that. Last night up at Martin Place this guy in a suit, I don't know who he was, came over to us with a box of donuts. I thanked him on every-one's behalf. Saying that to him would have made him feel good about himself, too.

There are a couple of coal-biters [beggars] you see with a [small box] and a sign saying, 'I'm homeless. I need money for food.' But their box is empty or they're close to making about $4 in change. He must be getting money on a [social welfare] benefit but you wonder where that money is going. It could be a drug problem or an alcohol problem. Why would you sit there with a sign saying you're homeless? What's it going to do?

There's a lot of us out there that are homeless but I wouldn't go around coal-biting. I think if I did that, got to that stage, it'd be a sign that I'm losing the plot. I'd only ask someone for money if I was five cents short for the fare for a bus.

I'm determined to do what I really want to do, but right at this time, where I am now [in life] is what I want to do. I feel that I'm stuck in a trap at the moment, because I'm getting too used to this homeless life (where homeless is a person with no home or a stable routine). You go to drop-in centres, have breakfast, find what you're going to do for the next three hours or watch television. Or go to the park and have your next shot [of heroin if you're on it] or go into the tavern and drink beer all day and come out blind. Or go to the TAB or the pokies and waste every last cent.

I've been in Sydney and NSW for about nine months now. I wasn't meant to stay here that long but things changed. It's getting close to the day when I'm out of here and the next journey begins. This is why I'm waiting around Sydney, for my tax return. I'll get a station wagon, a little cheap bomb, travel around Australia and do a bit of casual work here and there.

I've been saving money, a part here and a part there, but the rest [has gone] on smoking pot and drinking beer; no hardcore drugs [though]. When things get me down I might turn to drink or smoke a bit of marijuana. That's been worrying me, over-spending

Linz

[on drugs]. What I spent, I could have used to buy something else [instead]. If I stay in [the situation I'm in] I'll be part of the furniture and I'll get nowhere.

I want to better myself, be happy in myself. I've got go and get what I want, but it's not going to happen if I just sit in the corner at a [drop-in] centre watching TV all day saying, 'Aw! Don't change the channel! Leave the bloody channel!' It's a trap. I'm getting lazy. I get tired and I don't want to do anything. There was basically no more energy inside until I [finally] kicked myself in the head and went, 'Get out of here.'

One day, I will get off the streets because there's a future out there I really want. Like a fairytale, I want to wake up one day in a nice house with a nice wife and kids running around in the backyard. The thing is, I'm not going to get it coming to me on a plate; I'm going to have to work for it. That's what I aim for. I just write it down in a notebook and [plan] what I want. I'm stubborn and I'll take care of me own business. If I really want help, I'll ask. It's my pride. When I get to where I want to be [in life] I'll be able to walk out into the middle of the road and shout, 'Yeah, I've done it!' I don't care how long it takes.

Terry Balmer
age 33

I grew up in Marrickville, in Sydney, with my mother and two brothers. I didn't know me dad and me mum was an alcoholic, so I learned to drink from an early age. [I was] eight years old the first time I picked up a bottle of scotch. I grew up [where] it was the norm for me to hang around with me mates, get pissed and smoke some pot [marijuana], the usual deal.

I found a girlfriend and settled down from [age] seventeen to twenty-three, working all that time at a meatworks. I started becoming homeless after twenty-three. [What drove me over the first time] was just the girlfriend, really. It was [about money]. She wasn't happy with $300 a week; she wanted more. I was working two jobs, night shift at the meatworks at Botany and then I was doing four hours during the day at a pet care place in Taren Point. That was twelve years ago, so it was pretty good money, but she wasn't happy. Anyway, I'm not blaming anyone, but that's what set me going.

After we broke up I basically drunk myself silly for three months [while] staying on the banks of the Murrumbidgee River. I left our place and said to her, 'You keep the lot. I'll take the car.' I was drinking what they call goonie, $10 boxes of wine. I was drinking three of them a day. I could afford it because me and this other bloke used to camp out. I met him on the river and we put our dole money together. We'd just drink 24/7. [We would] wake up in the morning for a piss, have a drink for breakfast and then a drink at lunch. I sat there [on the river] drinking for three months until I woke up one day and said, 'Nah, that's it!'

I've gone through stints on heroin when I was a bit younger, before [I was homeless]. The last time I touched it was about seven years ago. I tried it when I was fifteen years old, got into it for about nine months and started to get a habit. My older brother found out about it and kicked the shit out of me, gave me a good flogging [and] taught me a lesson. It was better than any rehab!

I've also been in four rehabs. Once in Parramatta, and three times in William Booth [Institute run by The Salvation Army]. No amount of rehabs or anything can help unless you give up cigarettes, give up alcohol, give up food! It has to come from inside yourself. First time I went in, I went in for my girlfriend. I used the place once for a bed [because] I just wanted to get off the streets.

It introduced me to the streets and I've been off and on them [the streets] for twelve years. I've picked myself up, I've had jobs, I've saved some money. But one stuff-up leads to a culmination of everything, drugs, alcohol, gambling. I fall into the same pattern.

Terry Balmer

I've been in and out of homeless institutions, camping on the streets. I'm camping out at the moment. I've camped on the side of the road and in bus shelters, you name it.

I see what's going on in the streets. I'll tell you right now that country people help you more because they're not used to [seeing] so much homelessness. Whereas city people see it all the time and get hardened by it and just walk right on by. I was camping in Wauchope [NSW] and I was sitting near the river [when] a lady comes past. She was about fifty years old. She goes, 'You're camping out, aren't yeh?' I said, 'How'd you know?' She goes, 'I can tell. You're coming with me, I've got a spare room.' She put me up for three days. A fifty-year-old woman, she didn't even know me from a bar of soap; a country person, see. She had two young daughters and a young son and she said, 'I'm going to trust you to do the right thing, mate.' I've been down and out [in the country] and people have gone out of their way to go get me jobs. [They will say], 'Come on, mate, this is no good. You're not on the street any more. You come and get a job.' And they know someone who knows someone, you know.

On my travels [around Australia] something would pop into my head and say, 'go to this place', and usually I'll be working by the next day. No bullshit. Once I was in Murwillumbah [NSW] and something said to me [to] go to Roma, which is 800 kilometres away. I just hitchhiked there and the next day I started working at a kangaroo meatworks. Something kept saying to me all that day, 'Go to Roma.' I'd never even heard of it!

Other people from the country have given me work mowing their lawns. One bloke and his wife handed me an envelope for four hours' work. I thought, maybe $20 or $30; it was $150. These are real people. I've hitchhiked around Australia and the people who've picked me up are people who have been homeless or hitch-hiking themselves [so] they know what it's like. Yuppies haven't got an idea and they wouldn't give you a lift. I've seen them drive past ladies who need a lift! I mean, what's a lady going to do to you, you know? As I said, all the people that have picked me up on the road were once [in my situation] or lower class workers. I've never been picked up by a person in the upper class. Ninety-nine per cent [of hitchhikers] just want to get to the next town. [We want] no trouble. When I had a car I picked up all walks of life.

People are too quick to judge. We're all people and we all feel the same inside. Some are just in a better position than others. One day [those people] might find themselves on the other end of the scale and they'll think the same thing.

I've actually met a much better class of people and have had more genuine friendships on the streets than I've had at work-places. [With homeless people] everyone knows that you're an alcoholic or what your problem is. They tell you their story and you tell them your story and it may become a good friendship.

My philosophy on homelessness is there are four reasons that you're homeless: [either] you're an alcoholic, a drug addict, a gam-bler or you've got mental problems. I wouldn't say all [homeless people], but the majority. If you go out there and you're starving you can ask for something to eat and people will just walk right by. For instance, I asked this lady for the date today. She wouldn't even talk to me. I said, 'Well go on then, you snobby bitch.' The next person I asked was a labourer and he told me the date straight away. So what was her problem? She wouldn't even tell me the date!

They don't know the circumstance behind [someone's] homelessness. Maybe someone has been abused in childhood. I know a little bit about the issues that drive me to drink and drugs and gamble. There's something behind the [scene] that [a person's] got to deal with; maybe shame, loneliness, it could be anything. You just don't know. People don't know who I am or where I've come from [but] they make a judgement on it.

I'd rather talk to the bloke on the street; they're fair dinkum. The other ones are just keeping up with the Joneses. If next door's got a nice car, well, we've got to get a nice car. My girlfriend was like that. She always wanted the best of everything, to live like hobnobs, and I had to work two jobs to get it.

I've been through that many ups and downs. I might have to pick myself up three or four times during the year and then I go down for a month and then I'm back on top for another two months. There's another issue [I have now]. Because I've been travelling that long, when I get into a place, after two months I'm that bored that I want to see something new all the time. I've been travelling that long it's like a new issue has come into it.

There's still issues underlying it [my homelessness], though. I still haven't gotten over my older brother's death. My brother died when I was seventeen and that was really a big knock to me. He died in a street fight, three against one. He had leukaemia and his blood wouldn't clot properly. That was a big issue for me.

Also, another issue for me growing up was I started drinking when I was eight. I still remember why I did that. I thought, well me dad didn't leave when me little brother was born, he didn't leave when me middle brother was born but he left when I was born. I thought that growing up as a kid. Later on in life you learn there's two sides to a story.

I found out [that] when [my parents] broke up it was mutual and not just one of them. I found that out when I was twenty-three or twenty-four. My mum had to go for a psych evaluation after my brother died; she lost the plot a bit. I was going through all the family photos she had at the psych evaluation and I found out why they split up. It wasn't my fault at all, but you can't tell a kid that. My mum's not good on communication so, really, I would have preferred [after they broke up] to sit down [with her] drumming the real reason into me. But at the time she was working six days a week with three kids. I had to learn to cook for myself. My big brother kept me and the other brothers in line. So he was like my mother, father, best friend—gone.

Today, I still get angry and frustrated [at his death]. Not a day goes by that I don't think about him. The guys who did it to him got off. Money paid their way through. They were well connected with money and that. Even the judge [let them off without] even an assault charge on them. There are three [types of] laws in this country: one for the poor, one for the rich, one for the coppers. You learn all this sort of stuff as you go along. I see it every day and from what other people have told me and gone through.

I've got a lot of issues to deal with, anger about my brother, resentment [at life]. As a result of my ex-girlfriend I don't respect women as much as I used to. I've seen it, with me, that they don't want to know you if you've got no money. But as soon as I've got a job and I'm doing alright I seem to get a girlfriend no problem.

I'm hoping to get into forestry. I only recently came across a bloke who gave me a lift [when I was] hitchhiking who worked in it and he said, 'Why don't you go into forestry?' That started my idea to do it. A $1500 start, but it takes seven months' training to do it. For eight months' work [you can get] $75,000. Some blokes get $120,000, depends on the job you're doing. That's where I'm going, definitely. It's just getting those tickets [qualification certificates] in the first place. You need a ticket to do everything these days. Once I do that, I plan to work hard and get my act together and at least I'll have some decent money to do it.

There's no incentive for the poor people to work because you work for $400 a week [doing] unskilled labour [at] shitty jobs. You're only just surviving from week to week. It's not enough to get ahead, to actually put a deposit on a house or buy a car. Today, instead of looking at three months until you [can afford] a car, you're looking at three years. Some people can only put away $50 or $20 a week and it takes them ages and ages. You have to have good paying jobs or be able to get into good paying jobs.

They call Australia the lucky country—well it's becoming the unlucky country. In this day and age, if you're on less than $600 a week, forget it. The killer is rent, and food is so expensive now. Believe it or not, I see more rich people now than I did before. It's more noticeable. I don't know how people are keeping up with the Joneses: you got a new house, I want a bigger one; you got a Porsche Boxster, I want a Ferrari.

They have to get a better system for training people and some people have problems [and they need help]. Tell them where to get the good jobs and not just, 'Go out and work in manual labour or at McDonald's. That's their answer [to the problem]. They say, 'All the homeless are lazy. Go bloody work for the dole.'

Well, are you going to work for $12 an hour? Slave your guts out for that? I'd really love Bob Carr, I know John Howard wouldn't do it, just to come out and camp on the street for a week and just see how we survive. Put them on shitty wages and see how they survive and they'll be crying within a week. I'm telling you, it takes a lot of strength inside to live on the street, because your dignity is affected, your pride.

I'm sleeping up near the State Library, where you get people walking by. They look down at you. The first one or two nights I slept up there as soon as I see a couple of people I put me head under the blankets. But now I just don't even bother. Well, they're going to see me anyway. It's tremendous for them when they're earning eighty grand a year.

Instead of the government putting bandaid solutions on things they should actually get off of their arse and do something proper for people on the streets. Put infrastructure in so they can get good jobs, not shitty jobs on $400 a week. We don't want a handout; we want a hand up. Give them [homeless people] a fair go and train them properly. Fair enough if they don't want to work for $800, that is lazy, but there's no incentive [for those who need a hand up]. With $400 a week you're getting nowhere.

Another thing [for homeless people with addiction problems is that] because they're so relieved to get their [welfare] money, they blow it in one go and [they're] waiting a whole fortnight to get it [again]. It's the [same] cycle again, over and over and over. They need some incentives to break the cycle.

Now, after twelve years on and off the streets I'm conditioned [to it], but I still pick myself up and get a job and start working. With my brother dying and the break-up with my girlfriend, it's something in me that gets me back into drink and drugs and gambling. [I've got to] get over these things, over that hill. I've got to learn to accept the way it is. Like anything in life, you can't go back and change it.

I'm in my thirties now. Where am I going to be in seven years' time? That's why I better do something now. I just haven't thought that in the last twelve or fourteen years. I've been blind to it.

I'm starting to wise up. I'm going to try my best and that's all you can do, you know.

The government has to do something [about homelessness]. It's not an easy situation, but they have to do something. Like with the Housing Commission [flats]; who's going to go [live] in there? You're crowded in like sardines with thirty others in the complex and you're trying to give up the booze or the drugs or whatever and it's just all around you. Everyone's gambling and drinking and taking drugs around you. As anyone knows, if you want to get away from something, any addiction, you've got to get away from that environment.

There's not a town in the country where you can't score [drugs]. It didn't used to be like that ten years ago. Now, I can go into a town of eight hundred people and I bet you I can score that night, heroin, coke, pot—no hassles at all. In my opinion, even though I

Terry Balmer

hate the bastards and I'd never become a copper, the best coppers hail from these [city] places. They can see drug deals going down. I've seen drugs deals going down and [other] coppers don't even realise it. They're straight out of the academy and they just drive straight past it, they don't even know. Then they see a jaywalker and they arrest him!

[The public and government] need to treat people on the streets with a bit of respect and dignity. There are a lot of good people out there; they're just homeless, that's all. Give them a proper chance. They don't want the world, just a fair go.

Postscript

Speaking with so many homeless people afforded me the opportunity to understand the issue from the eyes of those people living on the street—it was both an experience and an education. Similar to the crisis facing Indigenous Australians and imprisoned refugees, homelessness is one of those social issues so large in it's scope and consequences that it becomes difficult for most of us to consider. Within a vacuum of understanding, the facts of the homeless issue are usually replaced by convenient social myths and stereotypes. As a result, the people who are actually homeless are obscured by the enormity of the issue and essentially become invisible.

Behind the worn faces and rumpled clothes of any homeless person, there is the real person. Someone as ordinary and extraordinary as any of us.

On the first day I interviewed homeless people for this book I sat in a city soup kitchen across the table from Davina Coad. The

Postscript

remains of her lunch lay before her as she spoke of the invisibility many homeless people suffer amidst society. She paused, trying to sum up the entire issue in a couple of words—a frustration I can now very much understand. Finally, her face sank into a deeply borne frown and she delicately said in a half-whisper, 'There's a lot of pain out there.' The words alone were a straightforward and eloquent summation of homelessness. But it was the non-verbal emotion that drove it home. It was said with such personal understanding, frustration and frankness that it has left an indelible mark on me.

The suffering Davina spoke of was one of the most confronting aspects of writing this book. Sometimes, the sheer depth and extremity of pain that people expressed seemed overwhelming. As a writer I felt that I had to maintain a sense of objective distance. At the same time, as a fellow human being, it was impossible not to be moved by the things I heard and saw. And yet, balanced against this sense of despair I also encountered many instances of wisdom, intelligence and circumstance-defying humour. Often, these stories came from some of the most fascinating characters I've ever met.

A great proportion of homeless people also suffer some form and degree of mental illness. For some it's a result of the situation they're in. For others it's a leading cause of their homelessness. For the past few decades many 'de-institutionalised' mental patients have been turfed out on the street with little or no support system. The more extreme of them are probably the most visible members of the homeless community; the ones you are more likely to see on a city street engaged in a heated argument with no-one at all. But as I mentioned, mental illness among the homeless comes in all forms and all degrees, from mild depression to schizophrenia.

Postscript

A sense of loneliness and isolation pervades much of the homeless scene. Yet in spite of it and because of it, many people living on the street manage to build a sense of community and support. I would often hear stories of homeless people looking out for others in the same predicament, whether they knew them or not. It could be a basic yet precious token of a blanket on a cold night or simply an understanding ear. We all crave some sense of belonging, a place where we feel at home. I witnessed friendships across differing age groups that were based simply on a shared sense of character or addiction.

Of course, for homeless people, finding yourself on the fringe of society is a strong enough commonality on its own. Many people I spoke with commented that their loneliness was compounded by the reaction they often got from members of the general public. Seeing as I spent a lot of time standing on the street or in a park talking to different homeless people, I was bound to see this first-hand.

On one particular occasion, I was sitting on a low wall near Sydney's Central Station speaking with an Aboriginal man called Jeffrey. Jeffrey was a man who'd lost all of his parents and siblings and was the last person left in his family. Each of them had died far earlier than anyone in a developed nation should die, from causes such as alcohol abuse, heart failure and suicide. He stopped talking at one point, trying to prevent himself from getting upset. As he did, I looked at the crowd moving past. I watched several people respond with polite distaste and even derision. At other times, the looks I saw were ordinary curiosity, apprehension or uncertainty. For every negative stare, though, ten times as many people walked past without even looking at us. From a homeless person's point of view, it's understandable how the memory of a negative look can make a strong impact and linger in their feelings the longest. A person's pride can only take so many beatings, whether heavy or light. It can drive a person further into low self-esteem and depression, disabling many of the abilities they need to get back on their feet again.

But how many of the homeless want to get back on their feet at all? This is a question I heard from everyday people I spoke to about this book. One of the myths is this: most homeless people wouldn't want to get off the street if they were handed the opportunity. I heard it often enough to warrant a reply, based at least on what I learned and observed.

It is true that some people cannot find a place in general society. For whatever reasons, they might choose to become drifters and members of the homeless community, preferring its form of freedom. From my experience working on this book, outside of a very small handful, most people wouldn't wish the homeless experience on anyone. There's very little romance in sleeping in a park in mid-winter with your arm looped around the strap of your backpack. As for those who welcome a homeless life, it would be even more interesting to find out what it is they dislike about life in general society that makes living on the street more appealing in the first place.

There are also those for whom homelessness has become such a part of their life that moving out of it can be as traumatic as staying in it. One person I spoke to had finally obtained assisted accommodation after waiting over a year. Long ago in his youth, life had dealt him enough blows for him to find solace in a beer glass. He was incredibly fortunate to get a supervised spotless apartment with a microwave, TV, washing machine and new kitchen. He was over the moon for the first few weeks, until he began to feel like a fish out of water. He missed the familiar security of the only family and friends he'd had in those years on the streets—fellow homeless men also fond of the drink.

As I write, he is currently struggling to not hand over the keys to the house and return to the only form of security he's known since the belly dropped out of his world. The temptation (alcoholism included) to join his old mates in the park is a strong one for him despite how much he hated being homeless in the first place. If he does return to the streets, it will have a lot to do with that human blanket of what's comfortably familiar and nothing to do with his particular dislike of microwave ovens.

But the majority of people I spoke with ended up homeless as a result of either a singular or cascading set of troubles or traumas. It's the memory of these troubles that seems to haunt their time on the street. A heroin addict isn't simply a heroin addict because he's a heroin addict. The same goes for others out there pinned in the vice of their own individual addictions.

Once a cycle of addiction and depression kicks off, many people find they simply can't cope, fighting a daily battle just to feel good about themselves. Pride, that sense of one's own worth, takes on a whole new meaning and preciousness for people living on the street. This is where the drop-in centres, food vans and refuges come into play. Their job is to try to help people get back up again and keep homeless people fed and clothed in the meantime. It's a task that includes the financial, mental, emotional, spiritual and practical kick-starting of a life.

Postscript

I am humbled by those people I met who, after climbing out of homelessness, decided to stick around and become volunteers, counsellors and social workers. You would think anyone getting back on their feet would want to get as far away from the issue as possible. Yet people such as Davina, Mike Reeves, Jai and Josephine felt a need to help and comfort those still struggling, even though they continue to work on rebuilding their own lives. Ray Brown is bringing his experience back to his people. Sallie connects with school kids and opens their eyes to the hard truths of living on the street. All of the contributors to this book have something that's not encouraged enough in society; they have the ability to refuse to be how society perceives them to be. They have broken through the stereotypes and myths.

The fragility and resilience of the human condition was constantly on my mind while working on this book. I saw countless minute acts of people looking out for others, not necessarily acts of heroism or romance. I saw people on both sides of the gulf doing what they could despite an unceasing tide lapping and sometimes lashing against their efforts.

Indeed, the resilience of the issue itself seems so interlaced with all the other issues dogging society that solving it, or at least eradicating the trap of homelessness, seems too large and complex a task. It was one of the reasons I asked the people I interviewed about what they thought needed to be done to solve the problem. Though their thoughts may not provide a solid strategy, there is certainly much that the government and welfare organisations can learn from the words of the homeless in general. They have an insight into the problem that no expert,

Postscript

no outsider to the issue, could bring to the table. From the many views and approaches I heard during the creation of this book, I believe it's well past time that homeless people were given greater input into the issue that affects them daily.

But that alone is not enough. Society and its governments must play their part by looking at homelessness not as a failure of individuals, but as a failure of policies and society. Many of the stories in this book give strength to the view that things can change.

Which brings me to a scene I observed during the first day of interviews on the street. It was a unique moment to witness, and although sad, it still makes me smile with a sense of hope. It was one of those brief, private moments where humanity shines through the cloud of society and you can understand precisely why giving a damn is not a waste of time.

I was sitting on a bench in Belmore Park, near Central Station, writing up my notes at the close of day when something caught my eye. Directly across from me, three male pigeons were trying to mate with a very subdued female pigeon on the grass. She hardly budged, and I realised she wasn't being compliant—she was dying. The other pigeons pecked her head a few times before finally wandering off under the curious gaze of some young seagulls. (Animals seem acutely sensitive to each other in a weakened state.) As the female pigeon was left alone, a homeless man I'd seen in Woolloomooloo earlier in the day was walking past among the city workers who were heading home. He stopped and looked down at the bedraggled pigeon.

The man wasn't much to look at, as we might judge. He was aged in his forties with a stubby build, a wild nest of sandy hair beneath a red, backwards-facing baseball cap, a tattered white shirt and scruffy cream trousers. But he was the only one who stopped. Catching the eyes of no-one and everyone, he looked around and held his palm out towards the pigeon as if to say, 'Look at that.' Then he took his hat off, gently tossing it like a coin onto the grass near the bird. It didn't flinch. So he stepped up to it and spoke to it. I couldn't hear the words clearly, but he was definitely coaxing it to get back up. No response.

He picked it up, examining it very gently. I could see its eyes were opening and closing sluggishly while he stroked its pecked head. Coaxing it again, he hoisted it into the air, but its wings weren't able to hold it aloft and it circled onto the grass more by gravity than glide. He gave it another, softer go with the same result. This time he sat next to it and waited, egging it on to get up.

After a while his shoulders slumped. In the end, he carefully tidied its wings, picked up his hat and stood, giving it one last imploring look. He walked away, occasionally looking back over his shoulder, shaking his head until he left the park.

Writing it all up in my notes, I left the park too and headed home.

Notes

1. Australian Institute of Health and Welfare 1999, *Australia's Welfare 1999 'services and assistance'*, AIHW, Canberra.
2. Chamberlain, C. and MacKenzie, D. 2003, *Australian Census Analytic Program: Counting the Homeless 2001*, ABS cat. no. 2050.0, Australian Bureau of Statistics, Canberra.
3. A Public Guardian is usually a NSW Government officer who is given jurisdiction to manage the finances of people with disabilities (sixteen years and over) who are incapable of making their own decisions. In addition, they may act as a substitute decision-maker in relation to medical and dental treatment.
4. A Proclaimed Place [PP] or Intoxicated Person Unit [IPU] is a place where intoxicated persons, aged 18 and over, can stay overnight.

The Regarded Degraded

I knew a place
Where the degraded
Are regarded
With love

One of them
Walks with a stick
Always spills his coffee
He's the community's aristocrat

Another always shows respect
His littleness is respected

Yet another gives out welcome
Makes sure he is welcomed
His fame it is assured

I know a place
Where the degraded
are regarded with love

Poem reproduced here with the kind permission of Davo Marsh. Copyright © David Christopher Marsh, 2002. A collection of his poetry can found at www.astreetspirituality.blogspot.com